Southern Living. GARDEN GUIDE

Herbs

Series Editor: Lois Trigg Chaplin

Text by Jennifer Greer

Oxmoor House.

Contents

©1997 by Oxmoor House, Inc.
Book Division of Southern Progress Corporation
P.O. Box 2463, Birmingham, Alabama 35201

Southern Living® is a federally registered
trademark of Southern Living, Inc.

Library of Congress Catalog Number: 96-67709
ISBN: 0-8487-2247-7
Manufactured in the United States of America
First Printing 1997

We're Here for You!
We at Oxmoor House are dedicated to serving you
with reliable information that expands your imag-
ination and enriches your life. We welcome your
comments and suggestions. Please write us at:

Oxmoor House, Inc.
Editor, HERBS Garden Guide
2100 Lakeshore Drive
Birmingham, AL 35209

Editor-in-Chief: Nancy Fitzpatrick Wyatt
Editorial Director, Special Interest Publications:
Ann H. Harvey
Senior Editor, Editorial Services: Olivia Kindig Wells
Art Director: James Boone

Southern Living Garden Guide
HERBS

Series Editor: Lois Trigg Chaplin
Assistant Editor: Kelly Hooper Troiano
Copy Editor: Jacqueline B. Giovanelli
Editorial Assistant: Allison D. Ingram
Recipe Editor: Julie Christopher
Garden Editor, *Southern Living*: Linda C. Askey
Indexer: Katharine R. Wiencke
Concept Designer: Eleanor Cameron
Designer: Carol Loria
Senior Photographer, *Southern Living*: Van Chaplin
Production and Distribution Director: Phillip Lee
Associate Production Manager: Vanessa C. Richardson

Our appreciation to the staff of *Southern Living*
magazine for their contributions to this book.

Thyme

Cover: *Rosemary, peppermint, lamb's ears*
Frontispiece: *Shakespeare theme garden*

Lemon balm

Herbs Primer

Herbs are so versatile and easy to grow that every gardener should have a few, whether tucked into flower beds, pampered in pots, or showcased in a special outdoor herb garden.

As practical as they are romantic, herbs are easy to grow and a delight to the senses. At one time, herbs were grown mainly for medicinal purposes and dyes, but today you can use them to enhance the natural flavor of foods, beautify the landscape, and add fragrance to the garden. They attract bees, butterflies, and hummingbirds, bringing you closer to nature. You can add harvested herbs to potpourris, butters, vinegars, and oils for charming gifts from the garden.

Most gardeners divide herbs into two major categories—culinary and ornamental—although some herbs often serve both functions. **Culinary**, or edible, herbs, such as basil, oregano, and thyme, add interest to favorite foods. If you are a health-conscious cook, use herbs as flavor boosters when preparing low-calorie or low-sodium meals. Once you have cooked with fresh herbs, you will want to grow them.

Ornamental herbs add color, height, fragrance, and texture to flower beds or to an herb garden. Excellent plants for landscaping, leafy perennial herbs such as artemisia provide a stunning background for bright flowers. Use ornamental herbs in flower arrangements and wreaths. You can also cook with a few of these herbs, such as scented geranium, lavender, and pineapple sage, which are prized for their unique flavors. But note, some herbs, such as artemisia, tansy, and yarrow, are not edible.

Most herbs are **perennials,** plants that go dormant or die back in winter and return in spring. Give perennial herbs, such as lavender, oregano, and rosemary, a permanent place in the garden, and harvest a little at a time through regular pruning.

Other herbs, such as basil, dill, and summer savory, are **annuals,** living only one season. They are planted and harvested in the same year and must be replanted every year. One popular herb, bay, grows as a woody perennial shrub in coastal areas where winter

The blooms of bee balm, an old-fashioned ornamental herb, attract bees.

Creeping thyme spills over a container filled with violas, boxleaf euonymus, and variegated edging boxwood.

freezes are not severe. In colder regions, the bay plant is treated as an annual and is *overwintered* (brought indoors for winter). A few herbs, including parsley, are *biennial,* which means they live for more than one year. However, you will need to replant biennials just as you do annuals every one or two years.

Most herbs thrive in full sun to partial shade and in well-drained soil. They need only a little fertilizer, watering, weeding, and regular harvesting or clipping during the growing season, which is why they appeal to busy cooks and weekend gardeners. Growing herbs is so enjoyable that you may keep adding new herbs to your garden.

As your herb garden expands, share it with others. Take a friend to your garden on a warm afternoon when the scent of basil perfumes the air, bees buzz amid the bee balm, and the blooms of yarrow wave their sunny hatlike heads. Friends will get as much pleasure from visiting your herb garden as you will from growing and using your own herbs, which is what this book is all about.

WHAT IS AN HERB?

The term *herb* is more descriptive than scientific and loosely refers to plants that have practical applications. Historically, herbs have been used for medicines, dyes, teas, seasonings, crafts, fragrances, botanical pesticides, and landscaping. As for how to pronounce the word "herb"—with the "h" silent or sounded—either way is correct. The British tend to pronounce the "h," while Americans drop it.

Culinary herbs can also serve as ornamentals as shown in this border of mixed basils, parsley, and flowers.

5

Herbs in the Landscape

The flowers, foliage, and fragrance of herbs combine to bring beauty to the garden as well as flavor to the table.

This kitchen garden offers a cook's collection of herbs such as sorrel, dill, sage, fennel, basil, and parsley.

One of the first delights you will discover when growing herbs is that these sturdy plants are often as attractive as they are flavorful. How you incorporate herbs into your garden depends on your landscaping tastes and the time you have to garden. Herb gardens may range from a few plants in pots to several plants in a specific, formal space.

Locating an Herb Garden

When deciding where to place herbs in your landscape, you will need to consider the following:

• Are you growing herbs strictly for harvest? You can easily grow large quantities of herbs for making pesto or for drying in rows in a vegetable garden.

• Is the site sunny? Most herbs will need at least six hours of sunlight. In the South, many herbs grow best in afternoon shade in summer.

• How do you want to work the herbs into your landscape design? Choices range from setting aside a formal herb garden that is the focus of a landscape to tucking herbs among flowers in a bed.

By the Kitchen Door

The most logical spot for herbs is near the place where you will use them—the kitchen. For convenience, plant a simple kitchen herb garden by the back door and harvest herbs often. Pruning helps plants produce new leaves.

Combine herbs with vegetables and flowers in your small kitchen plot for a handy source of herbs and other plants that you use in food preparation. In the South, many herb gardeners draw inspiration from colonial kitchen gardens, which were planted in tidy rectangular, triangular, or circular beds divided into sections of different annual and perennial herbs, flowers, and vegetables. This arrangement makes planting and harvesting easy, neatly pulls together an assortment of plants that look different, and gives the garden an attractive structure. You can achieve the same effect by designing your kitchen garden in raised beds.

In an Existing Flower Bed

Another easy way you can integrate herbs into the garden is to add them to existing flower beds. Simply plant herbs as you would any other annual, biennial, or perennial, changing them out each season. Herbs are so handsome and hardy that you may eventually convert the entire border to herbs, both culinary and ornamental.

Herbs with showy flowers, such as chives, make a good edging. In spring, you will have a delightful mix of colors when the chives flower with their pinkish purple orbs in a bed of bright bloomers such as yellow pansies. Use creeping oregano and creeping thyme to edge a walkway or even serve as a ground cover.

Herbs also lend seasonal color and texture. The dark leaves of purple basil are a good companion to the pinks of sweet William or petunias in summer. Fill holes left by spring perennials with transplants of annual, warm-weather herbs, such as basil and dill. When you grow herbs among flowers, use only pesticides that are approved for both herbs and flowers.

In a Perennial Herb Border

A perennial border of herbs is like a border of flowering perennials but emphasizes foliage and fragrance rather than flowers. A perennial herb border needs to have a vertical backdrop (a wall, a fence, or an evergreen hedge) to help the plants stand out.

With herbs, you will find that the most contrast among plants is produced by foliage colors and textures, and you will learn to appreciate the most subtle variation of leaf hues. However, your garden may have bold bursts of color from some flowering herbs such as Mexican bush sage, tansy, or yarrow, especially in the summer and fall. Borders are usually long and deep, but you may want to design smaller beds at first and focus on perennial herbs that do not have to be replaced every year until you learn what works best in your garden.

Typically, a perennial herb border is visually unified by the repetition of one plant or color theme, such as the repeated use of gray and silver herbs or of a flowering herb, such as lavender or yarrow. When you select flowering herbs, remember that color imparts a mood. Bright colors (red, pink, orange) are hot. Subdued colors (blue, white, gray) are cool. Also, consider the color of the background. Red bee balm would not look pretty against a red brick wall, but it would look great against a green or gray background.

Plant purple basil in a summer flower border to fill holes left by spring bulbs that die back in hot weather.

Add color to your herb garden by planting spring bulbs and flowers. Candytuft, columbine, dianthus, foxglove, pansies, primrose, and sweet alyssum are ideal in a perennial herb bed. They fill in the gaps while herbs are still sprouting in the spring. When the flower show is over, the herbs come into their full glory in early summer. Soft yellow daylilies with edible blooms are a good addition to the herb bed for early summer color and height.

Designing an Herb Garden

Larger, more definitive herb gardens have been a popular feature in European and American landscapes for centuries. Indeed, the combination of grays and greens, clipped and loose forms, fine and coarse textures, and subtle colors can make an herb garden as interesting as any other perennial garden.

Traditionally, outdoor herb gardens, or outdoor "rooms," have been formal, inspired by English and French knot gardens of the past. But a well-designed herb garden can also be informal, creating a collage of color, scent, and texture in a natural island, in a cottage garden, or in a series of stone-terraced beds. Which style you choose depends on the design of your house, other elements of your landscape, and the amount of time you have for maintenance. Just remember that a formal herb garden that relies on pruned hedges for structure will need more care, as diminutive hedges made from herbs require frequent pruning.

HERBS FOR ORNAMENTAL USE

Ornamental herbs are often grown as much for their good looks as for their fragrance or flavor. They are a good choice for incorporating into a landscape.

For flowers	Bee balm, chives, feverfew, lavender, Mexican mint marigold, pineapple sage, Russian sage, tansy, yarrow
For colorful foliage	Artemisia, bronze fennel, fern-leaf yarrow, garden sage, golden oregano, lavender, purple basil, tricolor sage, woolly thyme
For vertical interest	Bee balm, dill, fennel, lemon grass, Mexican bush sage, pineapple sage, yarrow
For edging	Annual/Biennial: Basil, parsley, sweet marjoram Perennial: Chives, creeping oregano, creeping thyme, dwarf garden sage, germander, lavender, mounding artemisia, prostrate rosemary, winter savory
For shade	Lemon balm, mint, parsley
For evergreen beauty	Artemisia, bay, germander, rosemary (winter hardiness varies with climate), thyme, winter savory

Informal Gardens

Some of the most inviting herb gardens are informal cottage gardens with simple but charming collections of herbs in curving beds and borders around the house. Design a garden based on the natural design of the land. For hillsides, terraced gardens with rustic benches and stone or pine bark paths are not unlike Mediterranean settings where herbs grow wild. Even if you harvest regularly, allow herbs to take their own shape in an informal garden, perhaps with creeping thyme softening the edges of beds and prostrate rosemary cascading over walls.

Formal Gardens

Knot gardens were popular in 17th-century Europe, where they were considered high garden style. They typically consisted of a square bed embroidered with a symmetrical pattern of dwarf or clipped, low-growing evergreen shrubs in varying shades of gray and green. The tradition of knot gardens still influences formal herb garden design. Here are a few popular patterns:

    • A circle or a square with a center circle intersected by paths that form a cross.

    • A checkerboard planting with alternating beds and pavers.

    • A circle or a semicircle with rays that divide it into pie-shaped pieces.

    By using beds and paths to create neat, balanced patterns, you can achieve the effect of French *parterre*—formal, patterned hedges that were inspired by knot gardens—without pruning and maintaining hedges. Enclose a formal garden with a fence, a wall, or an evergreen hedge.

Theme Gardens

An herb garden that features a specific theme can be fun to design, and you can use this theme as a way to separate a large collection of herbs into smaller, more organized sections. Here are a few ideas for themes or collections of herbs.

Informal collections of basil, chives, parsley, and other herbs perfume walkways and porches and embrace the landscape with gently curving lines.

Knot gardens rely on closely clipped hedges to create a symmetrical pattern in a neatly defined circle or square.

Divided into four quadrants with a circular bed in the center, this delightful retreat resembles formal herb gardens of the past.

Pizza garden. Try a small, raised, round bed divided into "slices." Pizza herbs include basil, chives, oregano, and rosemary. You may want to add several vegetables, such as cherry tomatoes and peppers. Since pizza gardens are a good way to get children interested in herbs, include a small clay pig for their enjoyment.

Tea garden. A tea garden is a collection of herbs commonly used in teas. Convert a raised flower bed into a tea garden by planting catnip, lemon balm or lemon verbena, peppermint, and scented geranium. Add a flea market teapot as an ornament.

Scented garden. While all herbs are fragrant, some have a most captivating scent. Plant fragrant herbs—artemisia, bee balm, lavender, lemon grass, pineapple sage, rosemary, scented geranium—in a place where people congregate. You may want to place a bench in this garden or install a gate that will brush across the plants as it opens.

Mediterranean garden. Adapted from the countries of the Mediterranean, a terraced design can accommodate a wide variety of herbs such as basil, fennel, garlic, lavender, marjoram, oregano, parsley, rosemary, sage, savory, and thyme. For height, add potted bay or citrus trees. Position a fig tree in a corner of the garden. Adorn the area with urns and pots filled with scented and flowering geraniums.

Salad garden. For fresh herbs to enhance a salad, plant this savory collection: basil, borage, chervil, chives, French tarragon, mint, parsley, rosemary, salad burnet, savory (summer and winter), sorrel, and thyme.

Literary garden. A theme may even be taken from literature. Gardens may house collections of herbs mentioned in Shakespeare's plays or in the Bible.

Shakespeare's references to plants in his plays provided inspiration for this graceful garden of herbs and flowers which includes dianthus, marigolds, yarrow, rosemary, and thyme.

Garden Enhancements

Statuary, potted plants, and other ornaments have long been favorite elements in herb gardens, adding color, height, and year-round interest. Details give a garden personality. Tuck small ornaments, such as those mentioned above, or other types of plaques or animal statuary in niches or under plants, so that visitors will discover them when they pass through the garden.

Garden ornaments. Today's garden ornaments can be family heirlooms or flea market finds. Here are some suggestions for using ornaments in your garden.

• Keep it simple. If there are too many ornaments in the herb garden, individual pieces lose their effect and the garden begins to look more like an outdoor curio shop.

• Place impressive features at the garden's center, near the entry, at corners, or in other spots where you want to draw a visitor's eye. These features may include sundials, birdbaths, urns, fountains, original sculpture, or architectural antiques such as an old gate, a chimney pot, or a pedestal.

• Add potted plants. A handsome pot containing a classic ornamental shrub or tree is a nice touch. Popular plants for pots include a bay tree, dwarf evergreen shrubs, dwarf fruit trees, and roses pruned into tree form.

• Set out old garden tools. Watering cans, rakes, and hoes can be arranged in nostalgic vignettes. An old wheelbarrow can serve as an effective centerpiece with herbs planted all around it. Just be sure to drill a hole in the bucket so that rainwater will not collect.

Garden structures. An herb garden is meant to be savored, especially on a warm afternoon when the fragrant oils are naturally released into the air. Place a bench or a garden table and chairs where you can enjoy the garden's view and fragrance. If there is shade, arrange the seating area there.

Arbors can offer vertical interest when covered with a grapevine or an antique climbing rose, and they can be shady niches for seating. Trellises also add vertical interest either when they are free-standing or attached to existing structures.

It is best to include benches, arbors, and trellises in your initial design drawing, so that you can be sure to designate the best space for them. Choose styles and materials compatible with your overall garden theme.

Place impressive features, such as a sundial, at the garden's center or wherever converging lines and attractive herbs and flowers, such as basil and marigolds, draw the eye.

A trellised shed gives this garden of roses, petunias, and rosemary a secluded feel.

Getting Started

Choosing the right plants and preparing a place for them in your garden are critical to your success with herbs.

The easiest way to begin an herb garden is to purchase transplants, but first find out what selections grow best in your area.

Perhaps the most difficult part of growing herbs is establishing your garden. Once you have selected the appropriate plants, provided the ideal growing conditions, and prepared a permanent site, your herb garden will be more fun than work.

Planning Your Garden

Before purchasing your plants, you will need to verify which ones grow well in your area. Most herbs grow well in all regions of the United States, and the exceptions simply invite innovation on the part of intrepid herb gardeners. For example, many tender perennials, such as bay and rosemary, thrive in Zone 8 and farther south but cannot take the cold weather north of that zone. If you live in colder areas, grow these herbs in containers and bring them indoors for winter. French tarragon does not like heat and humidity, so gardeners in the deep South grow Mexican mint marigold as a substitute. In Zones 9 and 10, certain perennial herbs, such as sage, decline in the hot summers. Gardeners in these zones know how to grow herbs as annuals in the fall, winter, and early spring. The Plant Profiles (beginning on page 47) will help you select plants that are right for your locale.

Laying Out the Garden

Once you determine what herbs are adaptable to your area, you need to consider whether you are growing herbs for culinary or ornamental use and what size bed you will need.

Size of the garden. If you choose to plant a few culinary herbs, a small bed, 4 feet by 6 feet, is all you need for the basics (one or two plants each of basil, chives, oregano, rosemary, and thyme). To have a little more fun, try a garden that measures 10 feet by 10 feet; this size can be divided into sections that hold a dozen culinary herbs (two or three plants of each), plus some ornamentals. If you want to grow a large quantity of herbs to use for gifts or to make a landscaping statement, plan a garden that is 20 feet by 20 feet.

Framework for the garden. When you have decided on the size of your garden, you need to sketch the design to scale on graph paper. Include everything—trees, shrubs, permanent beds, paths, edgings, hedges, evergreen plantings, focal points, benches, ornaments, potted plants, and enclosures. Because trees, shrubs, evergreen plantings, and perennial herbs provide the permanent character of the garden, be sure that you pay special attention to their placement. Remember to set aside spots near doors, patios, benches, steps, and walkways for fragrant herbs, such as lavender and rosemary.

Plants for the garden. Now that you have an overall view of the type of garden you want and at least a preliminary list of herbs, draw a planting plan to determine how many seeds or transplants you will need to buy. Sketch the arrangement of herbs on paper, placing taller plants toward the back and any low, creeping ones at the front. Remember to use perennials to provide structure and background to the herb garden. Use annuals to fill in seasonal "holes," or set aside a special place for annuals where they may be easily replaced in the appropriate season.

Allow for proper spacing so that plants will reach their full size; this spacing could be 1 to 3 feet for each, depending upon the herb. If you prune and harvest regularly, woody, branching plants will grow fuller.

Two or three plants are ample for most families' culinary needs. But if you are using herbs as ornamentals, plant them in groups of threes, fives, and sevens for more visual impact. (See page 37 to find out how to store the extra harvest for future use.)

A framework for your herb garden will help you arrange herbs and flowers that maintain seasonal interest, such as thyme, chives, lavender, iris, or other flowering perennials.

Selecting Seed or Transplants

You will find many perennial and annual herb transplants at garden centers, especially in the spring; specialty herb catalogs and nurseries provide transplants of harder-to-find herbs. Starting with transplants is easy, while growing perennial herbs from seed can be a slow process. It can take six months (or longer) for a perennial to reach the harvest size.

Seed. A few herbs are best started from seed because they are difficult to transplant unless the plants are very young; these herbs include burnet, cilantro, dill, and parsley. Such herbs have a long tap-root and may be stunted during transplanting. Some prized selections are not available as transplants and must be started from seed. Starting from seed is usually much cheaper, too, if you plan to grow large quantities of a certain herb. (See page 32 for more information on seed starting as well as other methods of propagating herbs.)

The following herbs may be started from seed, although many are also available as transplants: artemisia, basil, borage, burnet, catnip, chives, cilantro, dill, fennel, Greek oregano, lavender, lemon verbena, marjoram, mint, parsley, sorrel, and summer savory. Several selections, such as oregano, thyme, and some of the mints, have the fullest flavor when started from cuttings and transplants.

KEEP A JOURNAL

Save your garden layout and make it part of a journal. In this handy notebook, you can jot down selections of herbs that you want to be sure to buy again (as well as selections that did not work well). Include the time of year and any horticultural or design tips that helped make the herb a success, such as a pretty companion plant or the herb's ideal place in the garden. You may also want to note where you purchased the plants or seeds.

GOOD HERBS FOR BEGINNERS

The easiest herb garden to plant and maintain will include perennials that come back every year and require only watering, weeding, mulching, and harvesting. Chives, oregano, mint, rosemary, sage, thyme, and winter savory are good examples of easy-to-grow perennials. But if you want to use herbs in gourmet cooking, you will also need to set aside more space for annual and biennial herbs such as basil, borage, cilantro, dill, parsley, and sweet marjoram.

Transplants. Most herbs are easier to start from transplants than from seed. When shopping for transplants, look for healthy plants that are green or true to color (if they are blue-green or gray herbs). Avoid plants that are yellow, wilted, leggy, or flowering, as they are past their peak. Also, check leaves for signs of insect damage.

If you cannot plant the herbs the day you bring them home, make sure you keep the plants in top condition until you can get them into the ground. Place transplants outdoors in partial shade, with protection from afternoon sunlight, and water them daily. If they sit for more than two weeks, water them with a diluted fertilizer—but try not to delay that long before planting them.

Transplants are the easiest way to start new herbs such as rosemary in the garden.

Providing Proper Growing Conditions

When it comes to a permanent home, herbs do not ask for much. Basically, they need a sunny, protected site with good air circulation. The soil must be well drained, preferably be located in a raised bed, and have a soil pH near neutral (6.5 to 7.0) in most cases.

A Sunny, Protected Location

An herb garden needs at least six hours of sunlight. If you live in a hot area of the South or Southwest, however, the herbs in your garden will prefer their sunlight in the morning, with partial shade in the hot afternoon. The best site is usually on the south side of the house, since this exposure receives the most sunlight. Herbs, especially tender perennials, such as rosemary, also like to be shielded from the west and north winds. If winds are severe in your area, a building, an evergreen hedge, or a wall can serve as a windbreak.

Excellent Drainage

Good surface drainage is as important as sunlight to herbs. On sites with too little drainage, the soil can stay soggy, causing the plant

A collection of basils (purple, cinnamon, and lettuce-leaf) flourishes in a sunny, protected spot.

roots to rot. Drainage is especially important in the South, where humidity, high rainfall, and clay soil challenge the growth of Mediterranean herbs such as sage. A slope with loose, crumbly soil is ideal; the slope should be gentle enough so that erosion does not occur. Or consider building a raised bed.

Raised beds. If your property is relatively flat, the simplest way to improve drainage is to build raised beds. Raised beds are also a great solution to the problem of poor soil or rocky terrain that makes digging a discouraging (and debatable) proposition. A raised bed with about 8 to 12 inches of soil will suffice for drainage. But the most convenient bed height is 16 to 20 inches because you can sit on the rim while weeding and harvesting. And 2½ to 3 feet is a handy width; you can make a bed wider for ornamental reasons, but not so wide that you cannot reach the center from both sides. Remember, raised beds do not have to follow straight lines, especially if your garden is informal.

A raised bed provides good drainage for herbs such as garlic chives and artemisia.

Terracing. If your land slopes enough to erode or to be inconvenient for working, consider terracing the garden. Several tiers across the slope will provide well-drained, level areas for the planting beds. Low retaining walls made from landscape timbers, brick, stones, or other durable landscape materials hold the soil in place. A centuries-old method of gardening, terracing can be formal or informal and is as attractive as it is practical. (Before starting to dig, make sure there are no underground utility lines or large tree roots that might create difficulties.)

Terracing can turn a slope into a useful area for planting.

Building an Herb Garden

Once you have determined the appropriate site for your herb garden, consider adding some permanent structures. There is work and expense in building these, but your efforts can pay off with an outdoor garden retreat to enjoy for years to come.

Paths

In an herb garden, paths serve both a functional purpose and act as a design element. They provide access to the herbs and help define the garden's framework. Paths will handle the garden traffic so there is no walking in the beds and compacting of the soil. They may be hard surfaced, made with traditional flagstone, brick, or pavers (combinations of brick, tile, and pea gravel aggregate). Paths may also be made of crushed brick, pea gravel, stepping stones, pine bark, or pine straw. One traditional option regaining popularity is the grass walkway. However, a grass path requires mowing and will wear thin under a lot of foot traffic.

Working paths should be at least 3 feet wide to allow room for a wheelbarrow to pass. You may want to create a route for your wheelbarrow and make the main path more narrow, 1½ to 2 feet wide. These main paths can create a subtle extension of the herb garden if mats of creeping oregano, creeping thyme, or spearmint grow up around the path's stepping stones or pavers. These plants not only survive being stepped on, but they also release their fragrance when crushed.

Paths function as walkways for weeding, enjoying, and harvesting herbs. They also give a permanent form to the garden.

Paving can be expensive to install and to remove, so you should consider all options before making any decisions. You may want to start with temporary paths and make sure they work before committing to more permanent paving.

Enclosures

Traditionally, herb gardens were enclosed for a variety of practical and aesthetic reasons. From a design standpoint, if an enclosure is low and see-through, it can be friendly and inviting. If it is high and walled, it creates the impression of a private retreat.

From a practical standpoint, enclosures help keep animals out of the garden. They also serve as backdrops for herbs, climbing roses, grapevines, and espaliered fruit trees. They protect plants from the wind and cold, making it possible to grow more tender perennials and exotic plants, such as fig trees, which are classic herb companions. If your site lends itself to an enclosure, consider these suggestions.

Hedges. Hedges can be less expensive than hard structures. Good evergreen plants for tall hedges include cherry laurel, Florida anise, lusterleaf holly, Nellie R. Stevens holly, and wax myrtle. For low hedges choose from dwarf boxwood, germander, Korean boxwood, lavender, rosemary, and yaupon holly (in areas where it is evergreen). In a formal garden, you must prune hedges often.

Fences. Traditionally used to keep out animals, fences have character, whether they are white picket, wrought iron, or split rail. When choosing from the many fence styles, consider the shadows they cast and be sure that they are open enough to allow good air circulation.

Walls. Walls, be they brick, stone, or stucco, are the most expensive and permanent way to enclose an herb garden. They create charming courtyards where herbal fragrances waft through the air. In the humid South, a walled garden must contain intermittent open spaces for circulation.

Gates. A well-designed and thoughtfully placed gate can do much more than let people in and out of the garden. A gate sets a mood and adds interest, forcing the visitor to pause and enjoy the subtle colors or sweet fragrances of nearby herbs before entering. Gates of wood or wrought iron are ideal for herb gardens and can be combined with evergreen hedges or walls. Make certain that the gate is at least 3 feet wide to allow room for a wheelbarrow.

Fences enclose an herb garden while providing a pleasant backdrop for herbs, such as this bronze fennel.

A stone wall features pockets perfect for growing tufts of artemisia and thyme.

Materials

Brick, stone, and crushed stone are traditional materials used in herb gardens, but you should choose whatever best suits your home, landscape, and design. Always use high-quality, compatible materials when building beds, terraces, paths, and fences, and select one dominant material to unify the garden.

Brick. Brick has always been an attractive, traditional material in herb gardens, especially European or colonial-style gardens. Old bricks add extra character. Brick may be used in paths, raised beds, walls, and columns. You can probably build simple brick paths or raised beds, but large walls and hillside terraces may call for a bricklayer.

Stone. Cut stone or flat fieldstone is another favorite material in herb gardens. More than any other material, stone gives a new garden an old-world feeling. Stone is perfect for building raised beds, terraces, paths, and walls. Lay simple paths and low raised beds yourself, but call a stonemason for large projects.

Wood. Whether you use landscape timbers, dimensional lumber (2 x 4s or 2 x 6s, for example), or ready-made fencing material, be sure that it is a rot-resistant type such as cedar. (The wood should not have been treated with a preservative that is toxic to plants, such as creosote.) When building raised beds, anchor lumber firmly into the ground with stakes driven at least 18 inches deep and no more

Landscape timbers are an easy-to-install, inexpensive material for building raised beds that contain thyme, chives, other herbs, and iris.

The wide rim atop the raised bed enclosing this herb and vegetable garden provides a convenient perch for gardeners who have difficulty bending over.

Herbs have long been grown for their healing qualities, but horticultural therapists now tell us that the very act of growing herbs has healing benefits as well. People who suffer from aches and pains, who do not like to stoop, or who use a wheelchair for mobility can find hours of pleasure in an herb garden if it is designed for ease of use. Here are some things to keep in mind when planning this type of garden.

• Build raised beds 2 to 3 feet high so that they can be worked easily from a wheelchair; beds built 3 feet high can be worked while standing (without stooping). Make beds 2 feet wide or wider, but be sure the center of the bed is accessible. Add wide rims for sitting on while weeding.

• Locate the garden close to the house. Put it on level ground, or use ramps instead of steps on a gentle slope. Make paths 4 feet wide and hard surfaced for wheelchairs.

• Put a bench or a swing in the shade for resting and escaping the heat.

• Buy light, easy-to-use tools, and store them and other supplies close by.

• Install a watering system that is automatic or easy to turn on and off.

than 4 feet apart. Miter corners and nail in both directions (as you would a picture frame) for maximal strength.

Railroad ties. Use old, weathered ties, because much of their toxic creosote will have leached out. A single layer does not need staking for support but should be sunk into the ground 1 or 2 inches. To stack ties, bore holes through them. (You will need to rent an industrial drill for this.) Drive sections of galvanized pipe through the holes into the ground with a sledgehammer; overlap corners of stacked ties for strength. Cut ties with a chain saw; be sure to wear safety goggles and ear protection, and watch out for nails.

Planting and Care

Proper planting and care of your herbs will ensure a healthy garden and a plentiful harvest.

The herbs you plant are only as good as the conditions you provide for them. Granted, some herbs tolerate neglect better than others, but all do best with a simple, basic system of planting and care. Remember this five-part recipe for success:

1) sunlight
2) good drainage
3) lime (if your soil is acidic)
4) mulch
5) regular harvesting

Preparing the Planting Beds

The ideal soil for herbs is loose and well drained and has a pH that is near neutral (6.5 to 7.0). But such soil is rarely found around homes, having usually disappeared in the construction process. If your soil is heavy with clay or poor and sandy, be prepared to amend it with organic material. You may also need to add lime according to soil test results. (See Testing the Soil.) Adding sand to soggy soil will improve drainage.

An herb garden will thrive when planted and harvested correctly. Here basil is being carefully clipped.

Testing the Soil

A soil test determines the soil's pH, which is the degree of the soil's acidity or alkalinity measured on a scale of 1 (pure acid) to 14 (pure alkaline), with 7 being neutral. Most herbs grow best in almost neutral soil with a pH of 6.5 to 7.0. In soils that are strongly acidic or alkaline, essential nutrients are bound in the soil chemistry so that plants cannot absorb them. The United States Department of Agriculture Cooperative Extension Service offers soil testing services through its county offices or your state's land grant university. Do-it-yourself kits are also available from mail order sources, garden shops, and nurseries. Results of your soil test will tell you whether you will need to add lime, and how much, or supply nutrients missing from the soil.

Adding Lime

If your soil is too acidic for herbs (pH below 6.5), you need to raise the pH by adding lime. Lime can be added at any time, but the best time is in the fall (before planting in the spring). If this is not possible, work lime into the soil as soon as you know where your beds are going to be, for it may take months for the pH to change.

Breaking Ground

It is best to begin preparing your soil a few weeks before planting so that you can do the job in stages rather than all at once. Never work the soil when it is wet, as it will dry in clods. However, tilling or breaking up soil is easier if it is slightly moist, especially in the case of heavy clay soil. Water the day before breaking ground, or plan for your project to follow a light rain.

Break up the soil with a tiller or turning fork. Heavy clay may require a pick or a mattock. Work the soil at least 8 to 12 inches deep or until it is crumbly; this allows tiny roots to breathe and spread. If your soil is thin, rocky, or impossible to work, consider building a raised bed. (See page 15 for more about raised beds.) Fill it with a truckload of the best-quality topsoil you can find. Be aware that commercial topsoil varies greatly in quality and almost always requires the same amendments you would need for your own soil.

Improving Problem Soil

Herbs will grow in average soil, but they will not tolerate poor drainage, which is the main problem with clay soils. Although clay

Organic matter such as compost will improve poor soil. Add lime, if necessary, and slow-release fertilizer as well.

LABELING YOUR HERBS

Label herbs in the garden as you would jars on the spice rack. This procedure is especially helpful if you are planting new selections, for you do not want to lose track of your favorites (and failures). Some perennial herbs completely disappear in winter, and a label keeps you from planting on top of existing herbs. Many garden shops sell decorative labels that add personality to an herb bed.

retains nutrients well, it drains poorly and becomes sticky when wet. If you have clay soil, improve it by mixing 1 part native soil, 1 part builder's sand, and 1 part finely ground pine bark or compost. If you have sandy soil, you will find that it drains too well and is therefore low in nutrients. Add plenty of organic material—2 parts soil to 1 part finely ground pine bark or compost—to help sandy soil retain moisture and hold nutrients.

Planting Herbs

Most herbs love warm weather and flourish between the last spring frost and the first fall frost. However, a few cool-weather annual herbs, such as cilantro, dill, and parsley, can be planted in early spring and again in late summer for a fall harvest. (Check the Profiles beginning on page 47 for individual planting seasons.) If possible, set out transplants on an overcast day in order to lessen the shock from the sun's heat. Have fertilizer, hose, and mulch handy. Here is the planting procedure in six easy steps.

It is easy to start many herbs such as mint from transplants.

Step 1. Since it is easiest to start an herb garden by planting transplants, choose young, healthy ones. These are usually available in the spring and fall at garden centers. Local sources such as nearby public gardens and botanical societies also have special sales of locally adapted selections and hard-to-find herbs.

Step 2. Before planting, arrange potted herbs in the bed, following your layout, to see how they will look next to each other. Space them according to the size you expect the plants to attain. The spacing is typically 1 to 2 feet apart, but it may be greater for large herbs such as Mexican bush sage.

Label your herbs for easy identification from season to season.

Step 3. Add all-purpose, slow-release fertilizer to the soil. Or you can add organic fertilizers, such as cottonseed meal, bonemeal, or manure. (See page 25 for more information on fertilizers.)

Step 4. Water transplants thoroughly before planting. Handle the transplant gently by turning the potted herb upside down and sliding the plant out of its pot. To avoid separating the stem from the young, tender roots, do not tug or forcefully pull out the plant. If transplants are rootbound, untangle the roots to encourage them to grow.

Step 5. Dig planting holes so that plants are set at the same depth they are growing in the container; the top of the root ball should be level with the surface of the bed. Pat the soil firmly around the plant to eliminate any air spaces left around the roots.

Step 6. Water thoroughly, and mulch with 1 to 2 inches of pine bark to give your garden a finished look, to minimize weeding, and to help conserve moisture in the roots. (See page 24 for more about mulches.) Lavender, sage, and gray-leafed herbs prefer a sharp-edged stone mulch that does not hold as much moisture near the leaves.

Caring for Herbs

Once herbs are planted, they will need watering, weeding, and cutting back on a regular basis. You will need to mulch and fertilize only once or twice a year. If you provide this minimal maintenance, herbs will reward you with an appealing display and productive harvests for years.

Watering

Herbs need water several times a week after they are first planted. Later, as plants become established, you can water less.

How much water is enough? During the growing season, 1 inch of water per week is adequate. In times of severe heat or drought, however, you may need to water several times a week. You can measure 1 inch by placing several soup cans in the range of your sprinkler (or several pans under the soaker hose). Check your watch, and when the cans have collected 1 inch of water, check it again. Now you will know how long it will take to water your herbs.

You can sow the seed of the following herbs directly into the ground: Basil, bee balm, borage, chives, cilantro, dill, fennel, parsley, sorrel, and summer savory. Many will self-sow and come back the following year. Mexican mint marigold and nasturtium, which bear edible flowers, are also easy to grow from seed.

Thin seedlings to their final spacing when they have at least four leaves. You may transplant the thinned plants to another part of the garden or put them in containers to share with friends.

A watering wand or nozzle on the end of a hose makes quick work of watering herbs in containers.

You can bring water to an herb garden in many different ways: a sprinkler, a soaker hose, drip irrigation, or just a garden hose held over the plants. A soaker hose and drip irrigation help conserve water and do not wet the leaves; this is a good way to minimize the chances of leaf diseases, especially in the humid South. In the deep South, avoid watering during the hottest hours of the day (from 10 a.m. to 3 p.m.), or the herbs will steam-cook in the combined heat and moisture.

Mulching

Many herbs are shallow rooted, so a 2-inch layer of mulch will help them survive heat in summer and cold in winter. Mulch covers the ground like a blanket and helps reduce weeds. In summer, it keeps the soil from baking around the plant's roots, and in winter, it serves as insulation. In Zones 6 and 7, where erratic high and low temperature swings are common in spring and fall, mulch provides a buffer. Keep your herbs mulched at all times, but be careful not to pile mulch too thickly at the base of plants or the plants may rot.

Mulch also helps keep leaves clean by preventing soil from splashing up on the foliage. This is particularly helpful for culinary herbs and for silver-leafed herbs, such as lavender, sage, and woolly thyme. In addition, mulch creates a uniform texture on the ground, helping the garden look neat and clean.

Organic mulches, such as bark, compost, pine straw, and shredded leaves, build the richness of your soil as they decompose. However, if you use an acid-forming material, such as pine straw or bark, check the soil pH every second or third year to see if you need to add lime to neutralize the soil.

Be sure to keep mulch several inches away from the crown of plants so as not to invite disease. With gray-leafed plants, such as lavender, sage, and woolly thyme, place a ring of sand around the plant crown to ensure drainage; then mulch outside the ring.

Although it is usually easier to apply mulch after transplants are set out, pine straw is easier to apply before planting. Simply cover the bed with the straw, and as you set out transplants, push a bit of the pine straw aside to clear a spot for each plant.

A good layer of mulch will keep down most weeds. If new weeds sprout, pull them while they are still young. Do not allow weeds to grow too large; you might uproot herbs as you pull up weeds whose roots have grown larger.

Mulching makes garden paths look neat and cuts down on weeds. It also keeps herb roots moist in summer and protects them in winter.

Fertilizing

Herbs need only a little fertilizer, especially when you add compost and organic matter to the soil before planting. Here are some simple recommendations for feeding.

• Add an all-purpose, slow-release fertilizer to the soil at planting time. It will feed plants continuously throughout the season. Do not be tempted to use leftover slow-release lawn food; this contains too much nitrogen.

• In areas of high rainfall, such as Florida and the Gulf Coast, you may need a second application of slow-release fertilizer halfway through the growing season.

• After cutting a plant back severely for harvest, give it a boost with an application of liquid fertilizer or fish emulsion.

• Reapply an all-purpose, slow-release fertilizer to the soil each spring.

Slow-Release Fertilizers

Slow-release fertilizer feeds a plant gradually over a period of time. It is often called a controlled-release or timed-release fertilizer because it releases small amounts of nutrients at a time. The product's nutrients are coated and held in reserve to be slowly released over several weeks or months, depending on soil moisture or temperature. This type of fertilizer is ideal for the busy gardener because it does not have to be applied often (and it will not burn the roots of transplants.) The fertilizer must contain at least half of the nitrogen in a timed-release form. Organic fertilizers may also be considered slow-release, because they depend on the action of soil bacteria to release their nutrients. However, in warm, moist weather, when the bacteria are most active, the release of nutrients may not be slow. In this case, rich organic products, such as cottonseed meal or poultry manure, can burn plants.

Organic Fertilizers

Herbs are light feeders, making them well suited to organic gardening. The following is an easy recipe for an all-purpose organic fertilizer: 1 part blood meal, 1 part bonemeal, 3 parts wood ashes, and 5 parts seaweed meal. Organic fertilizers should be mixed into the soil—not simply spread on top—because they release their nitrogen as they decompose. Since it is not possible to mix organic fertilizers into the soil around spreading or matting herbs, you need to feed these plants once a month with a liquid organic fertilizer, such as fish emulsion.

When growing culinary herbs, such as these garlic chives, along with flowers, use only pesticides approved for herbs.

WINTER PROTECTION

Even hardy herbs may be damaged by extreme dips in temperature. To avoid damage by winter blasts, try the following:
• Do not fertilize late in the season. Fertilizing encourages new growth that will not have time to mature, or **harden off**, before frost; this new growth is more susceptible to cold damage.
• Apply 1 to 2 inches of mulch to the bed to protect the roots from freezing.
• Cover plants with an old blanket or a box on very cold nights.
• Screen herbs from winds with a hedge planted as a windbreak.

Pruning

During the growing season, regularly pruning healthy stems of most herbs will provide you with fresh cuttings to use in food preparation and as garnishes. At the same time, it will encourage your plants to produce new branches and leaves. Pruning will also:
• Remove dead or diseased stems
• Rejuvenate a woody plant in the spring
• Cause blooming plants to yield more flowers

Preparing for Fall and Winter

In late summer or early fall, make a complete harvest of summer annual herbs and a final harvest of warm-weather perennials. Although you may continue to snip mint, oregano, rosemary, and thyme through the winter, do not cut back these warm-weather perennials too severely, as this might promote new growth that could be killed by frost.

Tips for fall planting. Other chores that will pay off handsomely include additional planting and transplanting of herbs.
• Sow the seeds or set out transplants for cool-weather herbs such as parsley and winter savory.
• Divide bee balm and other clumping or spreading herbs, and dig up mint and other plants that can spread out of control.
• Transplant seedlings or shoots that may have sprouted at the base of plants, or pot these to grow in containers or to give away.

Fall cleanup. After you harvest the herbs, begin fall garden cleanup to ensure healthy plants for the next spring. Clean up all dead leaves, twigs, weeds, and flower stalks around perennial herbs, as these invite disease and insects. Add a 1- to 2-inch blanket of mulch, such as pine needles or bark chips, when plants go dormant in late November or early December.

Harvesting Herbs

How you harvest herbs will depend on your plans for using them. If you need only a few sprigs, simply pinch off some leaves or stems. If you want to harvest larger amounts, follow these guidelines.

In late summer or early fall, make a final harvest of herbs such as oregano (left) and marjoram (right).

How To Harvest Large Quantities of Herbs

• Harvest herbs on a sunny morning when the oils have their strongest flavor. The night before you harvest, mist or lightly spray herbs with a diluted solution of soap and then rinse with water. (Be careful not to splash soil onto the leaves.) Allow the herbs to dry completely the following morning before harvesting, and do not wash them again.

• Harvest leafy herbs before they bloom. The ideal time for more intensive harvesting of herbs is just before the plants blossom. Do not allow herbs that are grown for foliage, such as basil or thyme, to flower and set seed before you harvest them. If you cannot harvest before they begin to flower, trim the flowers away as they appear.

• Cut stems, not leaves. For a harvest of leaves, cut an entire stem. Do not be tempted to pick the leaves from the stem so that bare stems remain on the plant. In addition, regularly cut the stems to encourage branching. Take clippings of the tips (3 to 5 inches of each stem just above a pair of leaves) following the plant's natural shape. To harvest longer stems for use in oils, vinegars, or craft projects, cut every third branch, as if you were thinning a shrub. To cut clumps of herbs, such as chives, harvest the outer leaves a whole blade at a time by cutting them away from the clump at their base.

• Harvest herbs grown expressly for cut or dried flowers, such as lavender or yarrow, just as they begin blooming. By cutting flowers often, you may prolong blooming. Harvest flowers just as they are fully open. Do not cut back foliage on these plants until they have stopped blooming in the fall; then cut out dead material.

• Wait to harvest herbs that produce seeds, such as dill or fennel, until the seeds turn light brown; then cut the stalk. If you wait any longer, the ripening seeds will drop into the soil.

How To Increase Production of Herbs

• After heavy harvesting, feed herbs a liquid fertilizer.

• Avoid shearing a plant to the ground; the old woody base of many perennial herbs may not produce more sprouts.

• Do not cut herbs back too severely when the plants are under stress from a drought.

This flowering basil was not pruned and has set seed. You should always pinch the stem tips and remove the flower buds as they appear.

HERBS IN FLOWER BEDS

When you mix and match herbs and flowers, remember these three important "do nots":

• Do not plant invasive mints in a flower bed, or you may spend more time digging them out than enjoying them.

• Do not spray pesticides meant for flowers on or near herbs used in food, unless the product is also approved for food crops.

• Do not let flowers from prolific producers (such as chives and lemon balm) go to seed, or you will have bumper crops in your flower bed.

Growing Herbs in Containers

You can grow herbs in containers almost anywhere—in a garden, on a deck or a balcony, or even indoors.

If you are short on time or space, try growing herbs in containers. Place potted herbs on a deck, a patio, or a balcony as long as there is sufficient sunlight and water. In pots, herbs become portable, allowing you to place a few of your favorites in handy places, such as by the kitchen door. Then they are always in view and can be easily watered and harvested.

Herbs in containers are easy to maintain because you can provide the best potting soil, good fertilizer, and plenty of sunlight. However, they will need watering more often than herbs in the ground. But if you water regularly, you have more control over the growing conditions and can produce beautiful results.

Lemon-scented herbs, such as lemon grass, lemon verbena, lemon thyme, and lemon balm, make a fragrant bouquet in a pot near an entryway.

Healthy Herbs

First decide where to locate your containers. Because most herbs like plenty of sunlight, place them outdoors in a spot that receives at least six hours of sun (preferably not hot afternoon sun). Some herbs, such as basil, lemon balm, mint, and parsley, can take partial shade. Always remember that the closer your herbs are to your kitchen door, the more often you will use and enjoy them.

When using containers, you have many creative options. Place a pot of lemon-scented herbs near an entryway, use a rosemary topiary as a table centerpiece, or simply fill an empty space in a flower border with a pot of scented geraniums.

Grouping Herbs by Growth Requirements

When planting more than one herb in the same container, choose plants that need similar growing conditions. For example, Mediterranean herbs—oregano, rosemary, sage, and thyme—make good companions, as they enjoy full sunlight and thrive in nearly dry soil. Basil, on the other hand, does not need all-day sunlight and prefers more moisture.

An old dough bowl is host to bay, oregano, rosemary, sage, and thyme. These herbs like similar moisture conditions, making them good companions.

Mat-forming herbs, such as creeping thyme, Greek oregano, and winter savory, fit perfectly in the small pockets of a strawberry jar. Other herbs, such as cilantro, dill, and parsley, flourish in cool weather and make nice combinations for spring and fall.

Mint is better without companions because it spreads so quickly.

Choosing Containers

Your choice of containers is crucial to success. A container must have holes for drainage or the herbs will drown. In addition, it must be large enough both to accommodate all the herbs and prevent the soil from drying out too quickly in heat and drought, which stresses the plants. An 18-inch pot or larger is best for hot climates.

Test pots of various materials—clay, plastic, or concrete—to see what works best for you given your climate, the herbs you select, and your gardening habits. Herbs like the good drainage terra-cotta pots provide, but clay containers need to be watered more frequently in the summer and can crack outdoors in the winter. Shallow pots are handsome, but they, too, need to be watered more frequently. Self-watering containers hold extra water in a reservoir at the bottom so that you do not have to water them as often. They are convenient for gardeners who are frequently away from home.

If you are interested in growing herbs more for fun than for production, plant them in hanging baskets so that they will perfume the air near a doorway. You might not get bountiful harvests, but you will receive comments from admirers. Try chives, oregano, prostrate rosemary, thyme, or winter savory. With all containers, it helps to line them with damp sphagnum moss (before planting) as added insulation against heat and cold.

Basil and garlic chives flourish in this self-watering container which is ideal for busy gardeners.

Using Good Potting Mix

Always use a premium-quality commercial potting mix to fill containers. Garden soil is not suited for pots. It is too heavy and may harbor diseases and weed seeds. A premium mix is sterile, lightweight, and well drained yet able to hold moisture and nutrients. Look for mixes that contain quality ingredients, such as sphagnum peat moss, vermiculite, perlite, or sand.

A good mix is "pH balanced" so there is no need to add lime. It may also contain a slow-release fertilizer. Premium-quality mixes will lose their structure within a year in warm, humid climates such

This collection of different basils is kept close at hand so that the plants can be watered regularly and harvested with ease.

as Florida but may last two years in cooler climates. In general, fill pots with fresh soil every other year. Recycle old potting soil by mixing it into your flower beds or compost pile.

Planting and Care

Planting herbs in containers is easier than planting them in the ground because there is no tilling or bed preparation necessary. The perfect "soil" is simply poured from a bag. However, containers are also less forgiving if you forget to water or fertilize. It helps to place containers in a prominent location where you regularly sit or work outdoors so that you will always notice them.

Filling the container. Before filling the container, cover the large drainage hole with a piece of window screen or mesh, or with a coffee filter. This lets excess water drain and keeps the soil from washing through the hole. Fill containers to within 1 inch of the top. Work in a slow-release fertilizer if the mix does not already contain one.

Planting. Plant transplants at half the spacing recommended for the garden. If you start from seed, sow at the depth given on the packet. When the seedlings emerge, thin them to about half the suggested spacing.

Watering. Herbs grown in containers need watering more often than those grown in the ground. Do the "index finger" test until you know exactly when the herbs require watering and can follow a regular schedule. When the soil surface is dry to a depth of ½ inch, water the plants well. Afternoon shade also reduces heat and stress on plants in the summer.

Fertilizing. Because frequent watering washes the fertilizer out of the soil more quickly, you will also need to fertilize herbs in containers more often than you fertilize herbs in the ground. The slow-release fertilizer you worked in at planting should be reapplied after half the time stated on the package. (Three-month, six-month, and nine-month formulas are common.)

Dealing with seasonal extremes. Herbs in containers are more sensitive to changes in air temperature because the soil in a container warms or freezes faster than the ground. In spring and summer, you can expect plants to grow and mature faster. In fall or winter, the soil in containers will probably freeze before the ground does. Before temperatures reach freezing, bring tender perennials, such as bay, lemon grass, lemon verbena, and rosemary, indoors to overwinter.

Growing Herbs Indoors

Indoor herb gardening can be rewarding, but it is difficult to grow robust plants indoors year-round. If you would like to have herbs indoors for cooking or simply for enjoyment, consider the following plan. Have two sets of your favorite potted culinary herbs. Keep one outdoors in the sunlight for a week or two; keep the other handy indoors, where you can snip and use the herbs. Then swap the sets, so that each set of herbs enjoys every other week outdoors.

Most gardeners grow herbs indoors only in the winter months and take them outdoors for spring, summer, and fall. There are two ways to overwinter herbs indoors.

One way is to put them in a sunny window, in a greenhouse, or under fluorescent lights for at least eight hours a day and give them a cool temperature of about 55 degrees at night. Water them to keep the soil moist. This method allows herbs to continue growing while indoors.

When rotating two identical sets of culinary herbs in containers between the kitchen and the outdoors, carry them in a large basket. Here chives, mint, basil, oregano, and thyme are being rotated.

An alternative is to keep herbs in a slowed state or *stasis* by putting the containers in a cool basement or garage. They will go dormant but should come back in the spring. Water only enough to keep the soil from drying out.

You will need a greenhouse or an excellent artificial lighting system to grow herbs indoors for periods longer than six to eight weeks. Here are some herbs that will grow well indoors: bay, catnip, chives, dwarf basil, lavender, lemon balm, lemon verbena, sweet marjoram, mints, oregano, parsley, rosemary, sage, and savory. Be prepared to combat spider mites, which may appear on some herbs grown indoors in winter.

Propagation

Propagating your own herbs can be a simple task.

There may be times when you want to start your own herb plants. Often this is the only way to grow certain herbs for which you cannot find transplants. Or you may need to plant a particular herb in a mass planting, such as a knot garden, so starting your own plants is more economical than buying transplants. Whatever the reason, there are simple ways to propagate most herbs.

Seed

You can start herbs from seed indoors (in a greenhouse or a cold frame) or directly in the garden. Most herb seeds will germinate within two weeks and then need another two to four weeks to grow into transplants large enough to be moved to the garden. (See the Plant Profiles beginning on page 47 for information about when to plant specific herbs.) You should start your seeds approximately six weeks before the time you would set them outdoors. Here are guidelines for starting your own transplants in late winter or early spring.

- Use a sterile, lightweight soil mix specially formulated for starting seeds. Do not use garden soil, as it may harbor diseases that will cause seedlings to rot.
- For seeds that need warmth to sprout, keep the soil temperature at 65 to 70 degrees by placing the seeded flat on top of the refrigerator or the water heater.
- Fertilize seeds weekly with a half-strength solution of liquid starter fertilizer that is high in phosphorus, such as 15-30-15. This helps plants develop sturdy stems and well-formed roots by the time you are ready to transplant them.
- When seeds germinate, move containers to a window where they can get morning sunlight. When four leaves appear, move them to a larger container. Take care not to damage the tiny roots.
- Keep seedlings in bright light, by a south window, or under fluorescent lights. If the light is not bright enough, seedlings will be leggy and weak.
- Before transplanting, place young seedlings outdoors in dappled light for a week to give them time to adjust to the sunlight and climate. Otherwise, they may burn or be shocked in the direct sunlight.

Stem Cuttings

Another way you can start new herb plants is to root cuttings taken from stems. Look at your plant to identify the various stages of growth. Take a 3- to 6-inch cutting from a stem that is neither too young and

HERBS EASY TO START FROM SEED

Annual/Biennial: Basil, borage, cilantro, dill, lemon verbena, parsley, summer savory

Perennial: Artemisia, bee balm, burnet, catnip, fennel, oregano, sage, sorrel, winter savory

Diagram 1: Stem cutting

green nor too old and woody. This is called a semiwoody stem cutting.

Strip off the foliage from the bottom third of the cutting, and dip the cutting in a rooting hormone such as Rootone. Then stick the cutting about 1 inch deep into a container filled with a sterile potting mix. Set the container in the shade, and water the cutting enough to keep it moist but not wet. If the cutting seems to dry out, invert a glass jar over it to create a mini-greenhouse. (See **Diagram 1.**)

If you root a cutting indoors, place the cutting inside a plastic bag filled with 3 to 4 inches of potting soil that is sterile. Avoid soil that is not sterile, or the cutting may rot. Water the cutting enough to moisten the soil; then fasten the bag and set it in a north windowsill, where it will get bright but indirect light. Cuttings should root in 6 to 10 weeks (except bay, which may take three to six months.) No additional water is needed.

Diagram 2: Layering

Layering

Layering is a very simple way to propagate certain herbs that root easily along the stem. To start new herbs by layering, bend an outer branch of the existing plant until it touches the ground. Dig a small trench, and lay a portion of the branch (about 3 inches long) in the trench, leaving the tip of the branch exposed. Cover the part of the branch in the trench with soil, and anchor it with a stone or a brick. (See **Diagram 2.**) New roots will form where the stem is covered by the soil. After several weeks, trim the new plant from its mother, and transplant it to a new location. (See **Diagram 3.**)

Diagram 3: Layering

Division

Many perennial herb plants get larger each year, often forming clumps at the base or underground shoots that sprout up a short distance from the plant. These clumps and shoots make it is easy to get new herbs, or "starts," by dividing existing plants. Also, it lets gardeners quickly share starts with each other.

In Zone 7 and southward, division can be done in the fall, four weeks before the first frost. If you live north of Zone 7, wait until the first signs of growth appear in spring. To divide a clump, lift the entire plant carefully by wedging a turning fork deep under the plant. You may need to dig all the way around the plant to loosen it. Lift and gently separate the clumps, making sure each one to be replanted has roots and a piece of stem. (See **Diagram 4.**) Set these divisions at the original depth, and water immediately.

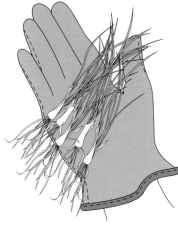

Diagram 4: Division

Herbs in the Kitchen

The pleasure of growing herbs reaches a peak in the kitchen, where the flavor of herbs enlivens foods.

Herbs have long been known for their curative powers. But they work another kind of magic when you use them to replace sodium and some fat products in your diet or to add new flavors and aromas to familiar foods. Once your herb garden begins to produce, you will enjoy cooking with fresh herbs, as well as storing and preserving your harvest for future use. Or use fresh herbs to create simple luxuries, such as gift vinegars, herb baskets, and wreaths.

Cooking with Fresh Herbs

The key to cooking with herbs is to use them judiciously to bring out the flavor of food but not allow the taste of the herb to overpower the food. The essential oils of herbs gradually infuse foods with flavor, and the longer the herb is in the food, the stronger its flavor. Because heat acts upon fresh herbs more quickly than cold, it is best to add most of your herbs about halfway through the cooking process. Bay is an exception; add it at the beginning of the cooking process and remove it before serving. When you use herbs to enhance cold foods, add them several hours ahead of time or the night before.

If you want to substitute fresh herbs for dried herbs, which are more concentrated in flavor, use three times as many fresh herbs as you would dried. The exception is rosemary, which should be used in equal amounts.

Herbs such as basil, chives, dill, and parsley are easy to chop and prepare. (Do this right before you are ready to use them for maximum flavor.) But small-leafed herbs, such as thyme and rosemary, must be removed from their woody stems.

When you want to cook with several herbs and spices, create your own bouquets garnis. If using fresh herbs, simply tie a small bunch of herb sprigs together and toss into soups, stews, or boiling water for cooking vegetables. Remove before serving. To prepare a bouquet garni that includes fresh or dried herb leaves as well as spices, tie a compatible assortment, such as thyme, marjoram, bay, and peppercorns, in cheesecloth and drop into the cooking liquid.

You can add fresh herbs to many of your favorite foods, creating simple, savory new combinations, such as sliced carrots with mint.

To make a quick bouquet garni from herbs, tie sprigs of fresh herbs to a celery stalk with string or a fruit peel.

Experimenting with Herbs

Experimenting with herbs is not hard. Simply taste an herb to identify whether it has a pungent, spicy, fruity, or floral taste—and pair it with a favorite food for a savory new combination. Remember, strong herbs, such as cilantro, oregano, rosemary, sage, and thyme, add quite a bit of flavor. Medium-flavored herbs, such as basil, dill, fennel, garlic, marjoram, mint, savory (both winter and summer), and tarragon, can be used more generously. Use delicate herbs, such as burnet, chives, and parsley, in abundance to taste.

As a general rule, add only a small amount of an herb at first, taste, and add more if necessary. When blending herbs, choose a leading flavor, and combine it with less-pronounced flavors. Never emphasize more than one of the strong herbs, such as rosemary or sage. Refer to the chart on pages 42-45 for suggestions about pairing herbs with foods.

Herb Teas and Other Beverages

Making herb tea is easy. Put a handful of fresh herbs in a teapot or a saucepan. Cover the herbs with boiling water, and *steep* (soak in liquid below the boiling point) for four to five minutes. Strain out the leaves, and serve this herb tea hot or iced with an herb garnish. Try mint, lemon balm, half lemon verbena and half lemon thyme, pineapple sage, or catnip (sweetened with honey) for a flavorful herb tea.

Herbs are also popular for flavoring other beverages. Add rosemary to lemonade, try mint with iced tea or lemon-lime sodas, or add basil to tomato juice.

Citrus-Mint Tea Cooler is an ideal beverage for summer entertaining.

CITRUS-MINT TEA COOLER

3 regular-size tea bags
2 tablespoons chopped fresh mint
1 cup boiling water
⅔ cup sugar
⅔ cup fresh grapefruit juice
½ cup fresh lemon juice
2 cups water

Place tea bags and mint in a saucepan. Pour boiling water over tea bags and mint; cover and steep 5 minutes. Pour mixture through a wire-mesh strainer into a pitcher; discard tea bags and mint. Stir in sugar and remaining ingredients. Serve over ice. Yield: 1 quart.

To extract the flavor of mint or other fresh herbs, add a handful to a saucepan, and cover with boiling water; allow to steep 4 to 5 minutes before straining. Use to flavor tea and other beverages.

Dianthus, pansies, and marigolds, all edible flowers, make a striking presentation.

REFRIGERATE HERB OILS AND BUTTERS

According to the United States Food and Drug Administration, unrefrigerated garlic in oil, butter, or margarine has been linked to botulism. The FDA recommends that garlic be soaked in vinegar before it is added to oil, butter, or margarine and that "similar herb or spice mixes" added to these be refrigerated and used promptly. Do not store any herbs in oil, butter, or margarine at room temperature.

Elegant Herb Sugars

You can add a gourmet touch to fruit salads and desserts with herb sugars. Try lavender, lemon balm, lemon verbena, mint, or rose geranium. Start with fresh herbs that have been washed and allowed to dry until they are free of surface moisture. Add them—with a drop or two of food coloring, if desired—to a cup of sugar. Mix in an electric blender on high for one minute or until blended. Package herb sugars in decorative glass jars and give with gourmet tea as a gift.

Herb Garnishes

Both the blooms and foliage of herbs and edible flowers make excellent garnishes, adding both flavor and style to your meals.

Chive blossoms look as lovely as a garnish as they do in the garden.

Soak garnishes in cold water for 15 minutes to make sure no insects or caterpillars are hiding in the leaves or petals.

For flowers. Try borage, chives, daylilies, dill, fennel, lavender, marigolds, mint, nasturtiums, and pansies.

For foliage. Try burnet, chives, cilantro, dill, fennel, lemon-scented herbs, mint, parsley, pineapple sage, purple basil, rosemary, scented geranium, and tarragon.

Herbs on Hand: Butters and Blends

Another way to cook with herbs is to mix them in butters and blends that you keep on hand and use in a variety of different dishes.

Herb butters. Use these buttery blends to season vegetables, meats, or breads. Any combination of herbs will do. For use with baked chicken, add marjoram and a little rosemary to butter or margarine. For grilled fish, add dill or lemon thyme. For breakfast breads, add mint or lemon verbena.

To make herb butter, beat 1 tablespoon of fresh chopped herbs or a combination of herbs into ½ cup softened butter, blended with 1 tablespoon of lemon juice. (If you use dried herbs, use 1 teaspoon of herbs, and soak them in the lemon juice a few minutes before blending with the butter.) Store in covered jars or crocks in the refrigerator for one to two weeks. It can also be stored in the freezer.

Herb blends. Dried herb blends make excellent salt substitutes or tasty toppings for salads, potatoes, rice, pasta, or bread.

Storing and Preserving Herbs

It is not always possible to have fresh herbs growing year-round. But you can store and preserve herbs to prolong your enjoyment of them. Herbs can be frozen, infused in oil, preserved in vinegar, or dried. Regardless of which method you use, always start with herbs that have been picked clean of dead material, washed, and allowed to dry until they are free of surface moisture. This prevents the growth of mold. The best time to wash herbs is the night before you harvest them. (See page 27 for details on washing and harvesting.) Check for insects or caterpillars after harvesting.

Basil, one of the most easily grown herbs, can be frozen or preserved in vinegar.

Storing Herbs in the Refrigerator

You can store fresh herbs for up to one week in the refrigerator. Wrap the stems in a wet paper towel, taking care to keep the herb foliage dry. Place herbs in a large plastic bag; seal it with air inside. Or, place long-stemmed herbs in a glass with an inch or two of water, and cover them loosely with a plastic bag.

Freezing Herbs

Although freezing preserves the fresh flavor and color of herbs, it does relax their shape and texture. This makes them unsuitable for garnishes but ideal for cooked dishes, some salads, and beverages. The following herbs retain their flavor well when frozen: basil, burnet, chives, cilantro, dill, garlic chives, mint, oregano, parsley, sorrel, and tarragon. Herbs can be frozen alone; in water; in vegetable, beef, or chicken stock; or in oil.

Just herbs. To freeze herbs, remove the leaves from the stems, handling them carefully to avoid damage. (Herbs such as basil will blacken if leaves are bruised.) Package small quantities of herbs in foil, and freeze in labeled freezer containers. Do not blanch or steam them first.

Freezing herb cubes. To freeze the herbs in cubes, remove the leaves from the stems. Chop herbs in a blender, and add just enough water or stock to make a paste; freeze herb paste in ice cube trays for use later in soups, stews, and sauces. Once cubes are frozen, take them out of trays, store in plastic bags, and label. Freeze combinations you frequently use, such as chives and dill; oregano (or basil), thyme, and Italian parsley; or chives, parsley, and tarragon (delicious in egg or fish dishes).

NO-SALT HERB BLEND

2 teaspoons garlic powder
1 teaspoon dried basil
1 teaspoon dried oregano
1 teaspoon dried parsley
1 teaspoon dried lemon rind

Process all ingredients in a food processor or blender. Store in a glass shaker (with a lid) with a couple of grains of rice or other drying agent to absorb humidity. Yield: about 2 tablespoons.

Note: This is a mild, all-purpose blend.

FLAVORED OLIVE OIL

2 large cloves garlic, halved
2 tablespoons white wine vinegar
1 lemon
1 (4-inch) fresh rosemary sprig
1 teaspoon whole peppercorns
2 cups olive oil

Combine garlic and vinegar in a small glass bowl; cover and chill at least 8 hours. Drain garlic, discarding vinegar; rinse and pat dry with paper towels. Set garlic aside.

Peel lemon rind in strips; place strips in a 1-pint jar with an airtight lid. (Reserve lemon pulp for another use.) Add garlic, rosemary, and remaining ingredients to jar. Cover with lid; chill 24 hours.

Let stand at room temperature 2 hours. Pour mixture through a wire-mesh strainer lined with 2 layers of cheesecloth into a decorative bottle or jar, discarding solids. Seal bottle with a cork or an airtight lid. Store in refrigerator up to 2 weeks. Let oil return to room temperature before using. (Clouding from refrigeration is normal.) Yield: about 2¼ cups.

Note: To use as a salad dressing, combine 2 parts Flavored Olive Oil to 1 part white wine vinegar.

Herb vinegars make perfect gifts because they do not have to be refrigerated.

Freezing herbs in oil. This is one of the best ways to preserve the fresh flavor of herbs. Add ½ cup vegetable or olive oil to 2 cups fresh herbs (leaves only). Place in container of an electric blender. Cover and process until smooth. Store in plastic containers, label, and freeze. Pesto, a popular product when basil is harvested at the end of the season, is frequently made and frozen this way. (See page 53 for a pesto recipe.)

Infusing Oil with Herbs

Herbs can be infused in oil for use in a variety of dishes. To ensure proper food safety, store herb oils in the refrigerator no longer than 2 to 4 weeks. Good herbs for infusing in oil include basil, garlic, marjoram, oregano, rosemary, sage, and thyme.

Preserving Herbs in Vinegar

Herb vinegars bring out the essence of the oils in herbs and make great salad dressings, marinades, and rich additions to cooked beans and other dishes. Since they do not have to be refrigerated, they also make charming gifts. (See page 116 for a tarragon vinegar recipe.)

Herbs frequently used in vinegar include: Basil (green, purple, golden), borage, chives (including the blossoms), dill, garlic, lemon balm, lemon thyme, mint, oregano, rosemary, savory, and tarragon. Combinations of herbs, such as a sprig of basil, cilantro, garlic, oregano, tarragon, and thyme, are refreshing when mixed with vinegar and then combined with oil to flavor a salad. Basil vinegar is a classic with tomatoes. Dill and garlic vinegar is a great mix for avocado.

A blend of lemon thyme and rosemary complements chicken and other meats; chives or marjoram vinegars are excellent in stews.

To make herb vinegar. Pack a sterile glass or plastic jar with herbs, either sprigs or chopped herbs depending upon the size of your bottle. A general recipe is 1 cup of fresh herbs per 1 quart of vinegar. (If you have washed the herbs recently, be sure no water is left on them or it will cause the vinegar to be cloudy.) You may also add other spices, peppers, and seasonings. Then fill the jar with vinegar that is at room temperature. Experiment with red, white, or rice wine vinegar and cider or other fruit vinegars, but make sure that the vinegar has an acidity level of 5 percent or above. Cap the bottle tightly with a cork or other nonmetallic lid. The next day, you will notice that the level of vinegar will have dropped slightly. Top off the bottle with more vinegar.

To store herb vinegar. Keep bottles in a cool, dark area. You can begin to use the vinegar as soon as it is infused with flavorful herb oils, usually within one week. Remove the herbs once the flavor has set in, or within two weeks. Pour strained vinegar into a sterile, decorative bottle. Tie a dried herb sprig around the neck of the bottle, and add a label to help identify its contents. Herb vinegar keeps about six months.

Drying Herbs

Drying herbs is the oldest and probably the easiest way to preserve them, making herbs useful for cooking as well as for crafts. Many of the culinary herbs can be dried and expected to hold their flavor at least one year. Ornamental herbs, such as artemisia, borage, feverfew, lavender, marigold, mealycup sage, scented geranium, tansy, and yarrow, also can be dried slowly in bunches and preserved for their foliage, flowers, or fragrance for use in crafts and potpourris.

You can dry leaves on or off the stems, depending upon their size and intended use. Small-leafed herbs, such as marjoram, oregano, rosemary, and thyme, are best dried on their stems. For culinary use, large-leafed herbs, such as basil, lemon verbena, mint, sage, and scented geranium, should be carefully stripped from their stems. You can use three drying methods: oven-drying, air-drying, or dehydrating. With these methods, you can determine that the herbs are dried when they

TANGY TARRAGON DRESSING

½ cup vegetable oil
¼ cup tarragon vinegar
1½ teaspoons fresh tarragon
¼ teaspoon salt
Dash of freshly ground pepper
½ teaspoon sugar
¼ teaspoon Dijon mustard

Mix all ingredients thoroughly. Allow the mixture to set 1 hour for herbs to impart their full flavor. Shake well before using. Yield: about ¾ cup.

Note: This dressing is great on a fresh garden salad with orange slices and nuts. It can be sweetened (add 1½ teaspoons of sugar) for use on melons or in a fruit salad.

Lavender, Mexican bush sage, yarrow, and other herbs and flowers can be air-dried in bunches.

are crisp or brittle like potato chips. To retain the flavor of the herbs, store the leaves as soon as they are dry.

Oven-drying. To dry herbs in an electric oven, place herbs on a cookie sheet, and set it in the oven on the lowest setting with the door ajar for several hours. Every oven is different, so stir the leaves occasionally, and test a leaf to see if it is brittle. Do not overcook the herbs, or they will lose their flavorful oils. It can be difficult to keep the heat low enough in electric ovens. If you can smell the herbs, they are losing their flavor. Gas ovens can produce better results. To dry herbs in a gas oven, use the same method; or leave herbs in the oven with the pilot light on for several days. To dry herbs in a microwave, place herbs between two paper towels, and microwave them at low (10% power). Turn small-leafed herbs such as thyme frequently. Experiment with the time, as it varies with the type and volume of herbs and with different ovens. Check your owner's manual for recommendations specific to your oven.

Air-drying. You can place herbs on special screened trays, and set them in a dry, dark, well-ventilated place, such as a closet, an attic, or a shed, for three to five days. Prop up the screen to let air circulate above and below the herbs, or toss them twice a day to help them dry on all sides. If you wish to air-dry herbs with long stems, tie them together with a rubber band, and hang a small bunch upside down for up to two weeks, depending on the thickness of the leaf. Again, pick a dark, well-ventilated place; good air circulation helps prevent mold. To improve ventilation, use a fan set on low. If it is a dusty place, wrap bunches of herbs in a brown paper sack or newspaper. Check the drying progress regularly.

To dry seeds of dill and fennel, gather seedheads just before they ripen; wrap bunches of seedheads in brown paper bags, and air-dry them upside down for two or three weeks. Then shake the seeds into the bags.

Dehydrating. Dehydrators used for drying fruits and vegetables yield good results for drying small quantities of herbs. Follow the instructions given for drying herbs. It usually takes two to three hours to dry them when the thermostat is on the lowest setting.

Storage. Dried herbs and seeds must be stored very carefully. Make sure the leaves and the seeds are completely dry, or they can mold. Strip the leaves from their stems, and store them whole (for maximum potency) in large, labeled jars (with both content and date) out of the sun and heat, preferably in a cool, dark place, such as a pantry or a cabinet away from the heat of the stove. Make sure the jars are clean, have tight-fitting lids, and contain no moisture; otherwise mold can grow. Check the jars in a few days. If there is moisture on the sides or lid, return the herbs to the oven to finish drying.

Affordable Luxuries from the Herb Garden

Many herb storage ideas—vinegars, dried blends, frozen pesto, even bouquets garnis—make special gifts. Be sure to add a note regarding storage (if refrigeration is necessary). It is also nice to add a recipe for using the gift. Here are some other ways your herb garden can enrich your life with simple pleasures.

Herb Basket

If you are in need of a quick, aromatic centerpiece or an easy gift, you can make an herb basket with four or five potted herbs. Buy young plants, or take cuttings of perennial herbs, and root them in potting soil in advance. For gifts, pot herbs in window boxes or other containers that are ready to use. Attach a notecard with easy care instructions and a favorite recipe.

For a useful gift, place several fresh herbs—thyme, parsley, oregano, or other culinary herbs—in small pots, and tuck them in a pretty basket.

Herb and Flower Arrangements

Some herbs, such as lavender and yarrow, are grown for their flowers. But others grown primarily for culinary uses, such as basil, dill, and fennel, have pretty blooms that will enhance any flower arrangement. For spicy bouquets, pair dill with wildflowers, chive blossoms with pansies, or rosemary with marigolds.

Guide to Cooking with Herbs

The following chart gives you some suggestions for using the culinary herbs included in this book. However, the fun of cooking with fresh herbs is in the experimentation, so feel free to create your own food and herb combinations. Just remember to use herbs sparingly; it is easier to add more herbs later than to take them away.

Herb	Appetizers	Breads	Condiments/Sauces	Desserts	Eggs/Cheese
Basil	Seafood Cocktail Tomato Juice	Pizza Herb Breads	Butter Sauce (for fish) Pesto Spaghetti Sauce Tomato Sauce		Cream Cheese Deviled Eggs Scrambled Eggs Welsh Rarebit
Bay	Aspic Tomato Juice		Champagne Sauce Marinades Pickles Spaghetti Sauce		
Burnet	Teas White Wine Cooler		Raita Vinegar		Cream Cheese
Chervil	Avocado Spread Cheese Spreads Tomato Juice Vegetable Juice	Herb Breads	Ravigote Rémoulade Savory Sauces Béarnaise Sauce		Cottage Cheese Cream Cheese Deviled Eggs Omelets, Soufflés
Chives	Dips Potato Skins		Herb Butters Vinaigrette Dressing		Cream Cheese Omelets Scrambled Eggs
Cilantro (Coriander)			Chutney Pickles, Relish Salsas		
Dill	Avocado Spread Cheese Dips Pickles Seafood Spreads Tomato Juice	Herb Breads Rye Bread	Mustard Sauce Pickles Tartar Sauce White Sauce (for fish)		Cottage Cheese Omelets
Fennel		Italian Bread Pizza Topping for Rolls	Mayonnaise Vinaigrette Dressing	Cookies Pastries	Omelets Soufflés
Garlic	Roasted Garlic Spread	Garlic Bread Herb Breads	Butter Sauces Pesto		
Lavender				Cookies Ice Cream	
Lemon Balm	Lemonade Teas White Wine Punch	Tea Breads		Cookies Custards Stewed Fruit	Omelets
Lemon Grass	Teas				

Meats	Poultry	Salads	Seafood	Soups	Vegetables
Beef	Chicken	Chicken	Broiled Fish	Minestrone	Asparagus, Eggplant
Lamb	Duck	Cucumber	Crab, Lobster	Mock Turtle	Green Beans, Onions
Liver	Turkey	Seafood	Shrimp	Pea, Potato	Peas, Summer Squash
Stews		Tomato	Tuna	Spinach, Tomato	Tomatoes
Lamb, Pot Roast	Chicken Fricassee	Aspic	Bouillabaisse	Bean, Broth	Artichokes
Ribs,	Stews		Court Bouillon	Chicken	Beets, Carrots
Shish Kabobs			Poached Halibut	Chili	Potatoes
Stews			Poached Salmon	Corn	Tomatoes
	Chicken	Mixed Green	Poached Fish		
			Salmon		
Beef, Lamb	Chicken	Beet, Egg	Poached Fish	Cream-based	Asparagus
Pork	Duck	Mixed Green	Shellfish		Beets, Carrots, Peas
Veal	Turkey	Potato	Smoked Fish		Summer Squash
Sausage		Tomato			Tomatoes
Meatballs	Chicken Kiev	Mixed Green		Chicken Broth	Potatoes
				Potato	
	Stir-fry Chicken	Black Bean		Chicken	
		Grilled Corn		Corn	
		Taco			
Beef	Chicken Pot Pie	Avocado	Fish and Shellfish	Bean	Beans, Beets
Lamb	Creamed Chicken	Coleslaw		Borscht	Cabbage
Sweetbreads	Turkey	Cucumber		Chicken	Carrots
Veal		Potato		Fish	Celery
		Tomato		Pea	Peas
				Tomato	Potatoes
Game, Pork	Chicken	Mixed Green	Fish and Shellfish	Borscht, Cabbage	
Sausage	Duck	Pasta		Fish	
Stews		Seafood		Minestrone	
Beef	Chicken	Caesar	Shrimp Scampi	Cream-based	Dried Beans
Pork	Turkey	Mixed Green			Green Beans
					Summer Squash
	Cornish Hens	Fruit	Salmon	Cream-based	
	Chicken		Shrimp	Shrimp	
	Chicken Curry			Thai	

Guide to Cooking with Herbs

Herb	Appetizers	Breads	Condiments/Sauces	Desserts	Eggs/Cheese
Lemon Thyme	Ham Spread			Cookies Sorbet	
Lemon Verbena	Fruit Drinks, Teas (especially Licorice Tea)			Custard Sauce	
Marjoram	Butters Cheese Dips	Herb Breads Stuffings	Barbecue Sauce Brown Sauce Fish Sauce		Omelets Scrambled Eggs
Mint	Cranberry Juice Fruit Cup Juleps Melon Balls Teas	Stuffings	Mint Jelly Mint Sauce Vinegar	Chocolate Candies Frozen Soufflés Ice Cream Ices Sorbet	Cream Cheese
Oregano	Cheese Dips Guacamole Mushrooms Tomato Juice	Herb Breads Pizza	Barbecue Sauce Cheese Sauce Mexican Sauce Spaghetti Sauce Tomato Sauce		Deviled Eggs Huevos Rancheros Omelets Soufflés
Parsley	Aspic Cheese Dips Guacamole	Biscuits Herb Breads	Cheese Sauce Spaghetti Sauce Tartar Sauce		Cottage Cheese Deviled Eggs Omelets Soufflés
Rosemary	Fruit Cup Paté Tomato Juice	Focaccia Herb Breads	Barbecue Sauce Tomato Sauce Marinades		Omelets Scrambled Eggs Soufflés
Sage	Sharp Cheese Spreads	Herb Breads Stuffings	Meat Sauce Pickles Tomato Sauce		Cheddar Cheese Cottage Cheese Fondues, Omelets Soufflés
Savory	Cheese Dips Paté Vegetable Juice	Herb Breads Stuffings	Fish Sauce Horseradish Sauce Tomato Sauce		Cream Cheese Deviled Eggs Goat Cheese, Omelets Scrambled Eggs
Sorrel			Cream Sauce (for fish)		Goat Cheese Omelets, Quiches Scrambled Eggs
Tarragon	Cheese Spreads Paté Tomato Juice	Yorkshire Pudding	Béarnaise Sauce Mustard Sauce Tartar Sauce Vinegar		All Egg Dishes Cottage Cheese
Thyme	Fish Spreads Paté Seafood Cocktail Tomato Juice	Cornbread Herb Breads Scones Stuffings	Creole Sauce Brown Sauce Herb Bouquets		Cottage Cheese Deviled Eggs Omelets Scrambled Eggs Soufflés

Meats	Poultry	Salads	Seafood	Soups	Vegetables
		Coleslaw		Chicken, Fish Tomato	
		Fruit			
Beef Pot Roast Pork, Sausage Veal	Creamed Chicken Duck Goose Turkey	Chicken Egg Fruit Mixed Green	Clams, Crab Halibut Salmon Tuna	Clam Chowder Mock Turtle, Onion Oyster, Spinach Tomato	Broccoli, Brussels Sprouts Carrots, Celery, Corn Eggplant, Peas Zucchini
Ham Lamb Veal	Chicken	Coleslaw Fruit Orange, Pear Tabbouleh Waldorf	Salmon Shrimp	Bean Pea Tomato	Carrots New Potatoes Peas Spinach Zucchini
Beef Lamb Liver Meat Loaf Sausage	Chicken Duck Pheasant Turkey	Avocado Bean, Egg Potato Tomato Vegetable	Clams Fish Lobster Mussels Shrimp	Bean, Chili Gazpacho Minestrone Mushroom Tomato	Broccoli Cabbage Eggplant Lentils Tomatoes
Beef Lamb Liver, Pork Veal	Chicken Duck Turkey	Aspic, Chicken Egg, Fish Mixed Green, Potato Tabbouleh	Fish	Bean Court Bouillon Meat Vegetable	Beets, Cabbage Carrots, Celery Eggplant, Onions Potatoes, Turnips
Beef Ham Loaf Lamb Stews, Veal	Chicken Cornish Hens Duck Turkey	Beef Chicken Fruit Lamb	Halibut Salmon Shellfish	Chicken, Fish Mock Turtle, Pea Spinach Tomato	Cucumbers Mushrooms Peas, Potatoes Spinach, Turnips
Pork Sausage Stews Veal	Chicken Duck Goose Turkey	Bean Chicken	Halibut Salmon Sole	Chicken Chowder Minestrone Potato, Tomato	Eggplant Lima Beans, Onions Tomatoes Winter Squash
Pork Veal	Chicken Duck Turkey	Green Bean Mixed Green Potato Tomato	Crab Salmon Trout	Bean, Chicken Lentil Potato Vegetable	Beans, Cucumbers Lentils Sauerkraut White Beans
Pork Veal	Goose	Mixed Greens	Trout	Cream-based Potato Rice	
Sweetbreads Veal	Chicken Cornish Hens Duck Turkey	Aspic, Chicken Coleslaw, Egg Mixed Green Seafood	Fish Most Shellfish	Bean, Chicken Mushroom Pea Tomato	Celery Root Mushrooms Salsify
Roasted Meats Stews	Chicken Duck Turkey	Aspic Beet Chicken Egg Tomato	Fish Most Shellfish	Borscht Clam Chowder Gumbo Pea Vegetable	Beets Carrots Onions Zucchini

Plant Hardiness Zone Map

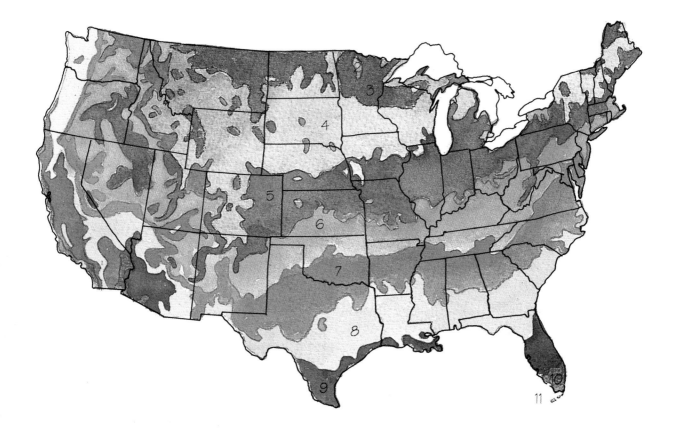

The United States Department of Agriculture has charted low temperatures throughout the country to determine the ranges of average low readings. The map above is based loosely on the USDA Plant Hardiness Zone Map, which was drawn from these findings. It does not take into account heat, soil, or moisture extremes and is intended as a guide, not a guarantee.

The southern regions of the United States that are mentioned in this book refer to the following:

Upper South: Zone 6

Middle South: upper region of Zone 7 (0 to 5 degrees minimum)

Lower South: lower region of Zone 7 and upper region of Zone 8 (5 to 15 degrees minimum)

Coastal South: lower region of Zone 8 and upper region of Zone 9 (15 to 25 degrees minimum)

Tropical South: lower region of Zone 9 and all of Zone 10 (25 to 40 degrees minimum)

Zone 2	-50 to -40°F
Zone 3	-40 to -30°F
Zone 4	-30 to -20°F
Zone 5	-20 to -10°F
Zone 6	-10 to 0°F
Zone 7	0 to 10°F
Zone 8	10 to 20°F
Zone 9	20 to 30°F
Zone 10	30 to 40°F
Zone 11	above 40°F

Plant Profiles

To help you select the herbs most appropriate for your climate and gardening style, the editors of *Southern Living* magazine chose 31 culinary and ornamental herbs to feature in this alphabetized encyclopedia. Chosen for their culinary qualities as well as for their beauty in the garden and for their usefulnesss in craft projects, these herbs are among the most popular with gardeners throughout the United States.

All the basic information you will need for planting, growing, and harvesting these herbs is included in the profiles. You will find a description of the herb; instructions for its planting and care; suggestions for its use in cooking, crafts, or the landscape; and guidelines for harvesting and storage. Photographs of each herb present a realistic view of the plant's size and growth habit, as well as provide ideas for ways to use the herb in the garden, in the landscape, or in a container.

For a quick overview of facts on planting, growth habit, and usage, refer to the *At a Glance* box accompanying each profile. The box contains the herb's botanical name to help you avoid confusion when purchasing herbs, as common names are not always consistent.

Although herbs are easy to grow in most climate zones, you will find that each herb has a different set of requirements. The profiles deal with these differences and any difficulties that you may encounter with particular plants, thus increasing your knowledge and your chances of success. You will find, however, a natural variation among plants which grow under different conditions. For example, flower colors are brighter in cool, crisp weather; plants often stretch taller in shade than they do in sun; and most herbs are shorter in hot, dry climates. These inconsistencies are a normal part of plant response, so keep them in mind when local information differs from what you read in the following pages.

Whether you are a novice or an experienced gardener, you will find that growing herbs is an education for the senses. Try your hand at planting a few of your favorites, and then enjoy their scents and flavors in your garden, in your foods, and in your crafts.

Create a miniature herb garden in a strawberry jar.

Artemisia

Powis Castle's frosty silver foliage will survive hot, humid summers.

Once used in medicines and liqueurs, artemisia is now grown as an ornamental. Its gray, green, or silver leaves provide a background for adjoining flowering plants. Dried artemisia is excellent for use in crafts.

In the Landscape

Artemisia varies in shape and size from mounding selections to woody, sprawling types that grow 3 to 5 feet tall. Its finely cut foliage contrasts with the coarser textures in the garden, and the silver-leafed selections are an accent among the predominant greens of an herb garden. Mounding selections are popular as edging plants, and taller selections are excellent in the back of a border. Artemisia is a favorite in silver-and-gray herb gardens. Poppy seeds sown in and around artemisia in fall or early spring yield a colorful combination in May.

Planting and Care

Artemisia likes full sun and hot, dry conditions. It needs well-drained soil with a pH of 6.0 to 7.0 for best results.

Start from transplants or divisions of existing plants in the fall or spring. Add a slow-release fertilizer to the soil before or during planting and repeat each spring. Space plants 18 to 24 inches apart, depending on the selection. You may have to stake or prune taller selections into shrublike shapes.

Perennial artemisias are hardy to Zone 4. In zones where the ground freezes, you will need to trim plants to the ground in fall and mulch after the ground has frozen. Remove mulch from around the base of the plant as soon as new shoots appear in spring.

Divide artemisia every couple of years in the fall. This thins out the root system and keeps plants from becoming woody and stunted. Fertilize the soil as explained earlier, and you will see your artemisia return the following spring with abundant new growth.

Propagate artemisia by division in the fall or by layering stem cuttings in the summer. (See page 32 for more about propagation.)

Species and Selections

The artemisia genus encompasses a large number of species, including classic French tarragon. (See the Tarragon profile on page 116.) The species mentioned here are ornamentals.

Artemisia Silver King *(Artemisia albula)* is a popular landscaping perennial with frosty, filigreed foliage. It can grow from 1 to

2 feet tall. Another selection, Silver Queen, is also a good addition to the herb garden. These plants spread, however, and can be invasive. To confine them, sink a bottomless container into the ground, or divide and replant in the spring. Silver King is susceptible to fungus in hot, humid weather.

Wormwood *(Artemisia absinthium)* grows from 2 to 4 feet tall and sports small, yellowish blooms in midsummer. One of the "bitter herbs" of the Bible, perennial wormwood was used for centuries in tonics. Both its leaves and flowers are aromatic. The hybrid Powis Castle, a feathery, silvery green plant, is the best artemisia for the South, where summers are hot and humid. It is also less likely to spread.

Southernwood *(Artemisia abrotanum)* grows to 3 feet tall, turning into a shrubby form. If you prune it to control its size and shape, this perennial artemisia will spill nicely over rock walls and edges. Its fernlike green foliage emits a fruity or medicinal fragrance and has long been prized for its ability to repel moths. Try the Tangerine selection for its pleasing aroma.

Use the Southernwood foliage to repel moths.

Sweet annual wormwood or sweet Annie *(Artemisia annua)* is the artemisia of choice in Zones 9 and 10, where perennial selections will not survive the heat of summer. Sweet Annie grows to 4 or 5 feet and produces lovely foliage that turns a greenish yellow. This plant reseeds prolifically. When dried, it retains its lovely, sweet scent.

Harvest, Storage, and Use

Harvest artemisia in late summer or early fall when little round buds form at the tips of the stems. You can use both the stems and flowers in crafts. Tie artemisia in bunches and hang it to dry in a dark, well-ventilated place. Make wreaths from the fresh foliage, as the dry foliage will be too brittle.

Troubleshooting

Leaves and stems are susceptible to fungus during hot, humid periods; fungus causes the interior of the plant to turn brown and die back. When cutting stems, remove those that will allow for good air circulation through the center of the plant. Trim off yellowed foliage.

MOTH REPELLENT

2 cups dried lavender buds
1 cup dried rose petals
1 cup dried artemisia leaves
2 drops jasmine and rose oil
Dried feverfew flowers

Be sure that all leaves and flowers are thoroughly dry. Combine all ingredients and package in a light net fabric. Hang around the neck of a hanger in a closet, or place in a drawer.

Artemisia flourishes in containers with flowers and other ornamental herbs such as salvia.

Basil

Pinch off basil's flower stalks as they appear, or the plants will stop producing. The flavor of the leaves is strongest just before the flowers open.

Basil is so easy to grow that even if you are a first-time gardener, you can reap bountiful harvests of this annual summer herb. The variety of selections, including several purple-leafed types, makes it a treasured ornamental and culinary herb. Basil's fragrance and taste are unmatched in salads (especially in tomato salads), in vegetables, and in meat and pasta dishes. Since basil is a tender annual, you will need to replant it each spring.

In the Landscape

Basil is a woody, branching herb that will become 2 to 3 feet tall and 2 feet wide, growing quickly as soon as the weather warms in spring. Although its primary place is in an herb garden, some selections are sought after for landscaping as well. Purple basil's deep maroon foliage contrasts handsomely with dianthus, Madagascar periwinkle, petunias, pink cosmos, and yarrow. Fine Green and Spicy Globe are bushy, low-growing, mounding plants with small leaves; they are excellent culinary herbs, but many gardeners also grow them as ornamental bedding plants. They are ideal at the front of a flower border to mask leggy stems and are great for filling holes left by spring bulbs. Because of their compact growth habit, they perform equally as well in containers.

Planting and Care

For best results, plant basil in full sun. In the South, however, basil benefits from afternoon shade. You can buy transplants at garden centers, but basil grows so easily from seed that you may want to grow your own transplants or sow seeds directly in the garden. Basil will not grow in cold soil, so you should wait to start your plants two to four weeks after all danger of frost is past.

AT A GLANCE
❖
BASIL
Ocimum species

Features: lush green or purple foliage, clovelike fragrance
Uses: crafts, culinary, landscaping
Type: annual
Height: 6 to 36 inches
Width: 8 to 24 inches
Light: full sun to partial shade
Soil: rich, moist, well drained, pH 6.0
Water: medium, water after heavy harvesting
Range: Zones 3 to 10
Pests: Japanese beetles, slugs
Remarks: one of the easiest and most productive herbs, good for containers

Basil likes soil that has a pH of 6.0 and is rich, moist, and well drained. Add a slow-release fertilizer to the soil before or during planting. Plant seeds in a shallow furrow and cover with ¼ inch of soil. Because basil seeds have a jellylike coating that makes them float easily, be sure to firm the soil to keep them from washing away with the first rain. When plants are 2 to 3 inches tall, thin them to 18 to 24 inches apart.

For an earlier start, sow seeds in flats six weeks before the last frost date in your area. Set transplants out when they are 3 to 4 inches tall, spacing them 18 to 24 inches apart. Basil transplants will not grow much until the days are warmer and longer, but then they will grow rapidly. You can sow them a second time in midsummer.

Basil requires little maintenance—only monthly clipping or pinching back to promote new growth and prevent seedheads from forming. If seeds develop, they will drop and may sprout the following year. After a heavy clipping, fertilize with liquid fertilizer according to label directions. Keep the soil moist, especially after harvesting, as dry soil can stunt growth.

Basil will often cross-pollinate with other selections of basil planted nearby, resulting in seedlings that may not have the same traits as the original plants. If you want your basil to propagate by reseeding, isolate each selection.

You can propagate small-leafed selections from stem cuttings and overwinter them indoors.

Species and Selections

Basil is so productive that you need to start with only one or two plants. You may be tempted to plant many more because basils come in so many popular types.

Sweet basil *(Ocimum basilicum)* is the most common basil selection. The plants grow 24 to 30 inches tall with leaves that are about 2 inches long and 1 inch wide. The foliage has a peppery-clove taste and aroma.

Another common selection, Lettuce-leaf basil *(Ocimum basilicum* Crispum), has larger leaves (3 to 4 inches long) with smooth edges and crinkled centers. This basil yields abundant foliage.

Bush basil *(Ocimum basilicum* Minimum) is a compact type of sweet basil. It grows less than 12 inches tall with leaves that are ½ inch long or less. These leaves are excellent when used fresh. Space

This collection of cinnamon, sweet, and purple basils yields a variety of scents and flavors.

51

Spicy Globe basil makes a striking bedding plant and an excellent culinary herb.

plants 6 inches apart in the garden. Bush basil also grows well in containers; try named selections such as Fine Green or Spicy Globe.

Cinnamon basil *(Ocimum basilicum* Cinnamon) is treasured for the cinnamon aroma of its leaves. Plants grow 12 to 18 inches tall and equally wide. They bear lavender flowers.

Lemon basil *(Ocimum basilicum* Citriodorum) grows 18 inches tall and produces light green leaves with a delightful citrus-clove flavor. Lemon basil reseeds easily. Named selections include Mrs. Burns' Lemon Basil, which is more robust and has larger leaves.

Purple basil comes in several selections. Purple Ruffles *(Ocimum basilicum* Purple Ruffles) and Dark Opal *(Ocimum basilicum* Purpurascens) are selections of sweet basil with large maroon to purplish leaves and lavender blossoms. Their scent and flavor are not as sweet as those of other basils. But when the leaves are added to white vinegar, they turn the vinegar pink. A dwarf selection of Purple Ruffles is also available. It is popular for adding foliage color to flower gardens. Plant this basil in partial shade.

Thai basil *(Ocimum basilicum* Siam Queen) is an All-America selections winner prized for its ability to yield a good harvest and its tendency to flower later than other basils. It grows 2 to 3 feet tall and about 2 feet wide.

Harvest, Storage, and Use

When you want to use basil fresh from the garden, cut the tips of the stems as you need the leaves. Wait until young plants grow to at least 6 inches tall; this will encourage branching. To extend the life of the plants, pinch off the flower buds as they appear in July and August. If you do not pinch off the flowers, the plant will stop producing new leaves. You should be able to make several harvests in one season before frost kills the plants. If you allow a plant to become covered with seedheads, clip them off and use the leaves to make a basil wreath.

Basil can be dried, as can most herbs, with some of its aroma preserved. However, its flavor is best preserved by freezing or by storing the leaves in vinegars or refrigerated oils. Handle leaves gingerly, or they will bruise and blacken. Harvest basil just before the flower buds are ready to open; clip the plant back to one-third its original size.

Use fresh basil in soups, pasta dishes, and pesto and with cucumbers, eggs, and shrimp. To benefit from basil's full flavor, add it during the last 10 minutes of cooking. For an interesting garnish, add strips of sliced basil leaves to canned soups or stews just before serving. Basil blends well with oregano, parsley, rosemary, sage, and thyme.

SURPRISING BASILS

The many scents and forms of basil offer an exciting assortment.

Bush basil
Cinnamon basil
Lemon basil
Lettuce-leaf basil
Purple basil
Sweet basil
Thai basil

PESTO

4 cloves garlic
2 tablespoons pine nuts
1½ cups tightly packed fresh basil leaves
½ cup chopped fresh parsley
⅓ cup freshly grated Parmesan cheese
½ cup commercial Italian dressing

Position knife blade in food processor bowl. Drop garlic and pine nuts through food chute with processor running; process 5 seconds or until garlic is minced. Add basil and parsley; process 10 seconds or until minced. Add cheese; process until blended. Slowly pour Italian dressing through food chute with processor running, blending until smooth. Yield: 1 cup plus 2 tablespoons.

Note: Serve over hot pasta, spread on chicken or fish before cooking, use as stuffing for mushroom caps, or spread on fresh tomato slices or baguette slices.

Troubleshooting

Keep basil healthy with regular pruning to remove flowers and seedheads. When cutting, be careful not to cut back to the woody stem, or the plant may not recover. Basil is occasionally bothered by slugs or Japanese beetles. See pages 124-125 for more about these pests.

Bay

Bay is evergreen, so you can pick its aromatic leaves as you need them for use in soups, sauces, and vegetables. You can also easily dry leaves for crafts.

Sweet bay, as the plant is often called, is a handsome, shrublike, semitropical tree with evergreen, glossy foliage. Mentioned in Greek and Roman legends, bay was once used to make laurels for honoring poets and athletes. Today herb gardeners prize bay as a flavorful ingredient in soups, stews, and herb and spice blends. It can be grown in a container or in the ground in areas with mild winters.

In the Landscape

In Zone 8 and farther south, bay can become an impressive landscape tree, growing from 6 to 30 feet tall. Its shape makes it ideal as an informal screen or sheared hedge.

Bay is also an elegant container plant, growing a few inches each year and reaching 4 to 6 feet tall. Bay planted in containers has a variety of decorative landscape uses. Prune the tree to complement a formal design or train it to form a topiary. Use it to fill an empty corner of a terrace or frame an entrance. Bay nicely anchors a container or patio herb garden, providing height when smaller herbs are grouped around its base.

Planting and Care

Bay likes a sunny site, preferably protected by a building or a wall. Plant it in rich, well-drained soil with a pH of 6.0. For quickest results, start with a small plant from a nursery. Add a slow-release fertilizer to the soil before or during planting. Be careful not to overwater; let the soil dry out between waterings. You can move bay in a container outdoors in the summer. If you plant bay in a clay pot, you can sink it into the ground until fall to cut down on watering during summer months. Bring potted bay indoors as soon as the weather starts to turn cold. Place it in a cool, sunny room or in a cold frame or greenhouse for the winter.

Mature trees planted outdoors may survive overnight temperature dips to 10 to 15 degrees if they are planted where heat reflected from a wall will keep the plant a few degrees warmer. In the middle and lower South, frozen plants should sprout from the roots the following spring, but it may take years for them to return to their previous size. Feed trees with slow-release fertilizer in March and August.

AT A GLANCE
❖
BAY
Laurus nobilis

Features: evergreen, shrublike tree with glossy leaves

Uses: crafts, culinary, landscaping

Type: perennial

Height: 4 to 6 feet in containers, to 30 feet outdoors

Width: 3 feet in containers, 10 feet outdoors

Light: full or filtered sun

Soil: rich, well drained, pH 6.0

Water: low

Range: Zone 4 to 10 in containers, hardy in Zones 9 and 10

Pests: scales

Remarks: shelter from cold winds and hot afternoon sun, do not overwater

Start from cuttings of the tips in three to six months, but avoid fresh, new growth as it will not root. Pinch off some of the tips in early summer or late fall. To encourage rooting, gently scrape the bark off opposite sides of the bottom stem to expose the green *cambium,* or growth layer, just below the bark. (See page 32 for more information on propagation.)

Species and Selections

Bay *(Laurus nobilis)* sometimes is called true laurel. Do not confuse it with red bay *(Persea borbonia),* a native Southern tree whose leaves are often used as a milder substitute for bay. The dried leaves of California bay *(Umbellularia californica)* are occasionally available in supermarkets; their flavor is different and much stronger than that of *Laurus nobilis.*

Harvest, Storage, and Use

You may harvest bay leaves year-round. Carefully pinch the mature leaves from their woody stems; avoid stripping the bark. Use fresh or dried bay leaves in soups, stews, vegetables, herb blends, bouquets garnis, or potpourris. Remember that fresh leaves are stronger and more aromatic than dry leaves, so use them sparingly. When drying bay leaves, take them off the stem, cover with a towel, and place books on top to flatten the leaves. Remove the books after one week.

Troubleshooting

Bay is occasionally attacked by scales. Scales may be soft- or hard-bodied insects that cling to the underside of leaves and along stems, sucking the sap from bay.

It is important to control scales when they first appear and while they are looking for a place to feed; they are harder to kill as they get older. The eggs are naturally resistant to pesticides, so you must spray more than once to kill young scales as they emerge. In winter, spray bay's branches with dormant oil to smother the eggs, preventing them from hatching in spring.

A semitropical tree, bay is usually grown in a container to make it easy to bring indoors in winter.

MASHED POTATOES WITH BAY

2 pounds baking potatoes, peeled and cut into ¾-inch pieces
2 cups water
2 bay leaves
¼ cup butter or margarine
¼ cup milk
½ teaspoon salt

Combine first 3 ingredients in a medium saucepan. Bring to a boil; cover, reduce heat, and simmer 15 to 20 minutes or until potato is tender. Remove and discard bay leaves. Drain potato, reserving ¼ cup cooking liquid.

Combine potato, reserved liquid, butter, milk, and salt in a medium bowl. Beat at medium speed of an electric mixer until fluffy. Yield: 4 servings.

Bee Balm

Bee balm's sweet-smelling flowers attract bees, butterflies, and hummingbirds.

Topped with white, scarlet, or pink blooms that look like mopheads, bee balm brings color to the summer herb garden; in addition, its leaves release a heady aroma of orange and spice. A native of the eastern United States, bee balm was used in a tea made by the Oswego Indians. As its name implies, bee balm is best known for attracting bees (and butterflies and hummingbirds) to the garden.

In the Landscape

Bee balm forms an upright, branching, shrublike plant 2 to 4 feet tall. It should be planted in mass as its flowers are open and airy. Use it at the back of a perennial border, in a wildflower garden, or in front of an evergreen hedge. Red selections are among the best plants for attracting hummingbirds.

Planting and Care

Plant bee balm in full sun or partial shade. The fastest way to start bee balm is from transplants set out in fall or spring. Be aware, however, that young plants may take a year to bloom. Bee balm is also easy to start from divisions taken from a large clump in fall or spring.

For a bushier shrub, pinch back the top as the plant grows. Harvesting flowers when they first appear in summer will promote a second round of blooms on healthier plants. In the fall, cut plants back to within several inches of the ground.

Bee balm likes rich, well-drained soil with a pH of 6.0 to 6.7; amend soil with organic matter. Add a slow-release fertilizer to the soil before planting and again the following spring. Give bee balm ample moisture, and never allow the soil to dry out. Be sure to mulch plants in the spring.

Once established, bee balm easily spreads by runners and seeds and may spread out of bounds. However, dividing plants every three or four years will rejuvenate them and keep them from spreading too far. Often the roots and stems from the original plant will be dead at the center of the planting; dig and replant new sprouts growing from the roots at the edge of the clump.

Species and Selections

Bee balm (*Monarda didyma*) and its hybrids come in a variety of colors. Panorama offers feathery flowers in shades of pink, salmon, and crimson. Lambada features lavender blooms and is resistant to mildew. Gardenview Scarlet is brilliant red and also resists mildew.

AT A GLANCE
❖
BEE BALM
Monarda species

Features: tall plant with colorful, showy flowers

Uses: crafts, culinary, landscaping

Type: perennial

Height: 2 to 4 feet

Width: 1½ to 2 feet

Light: full sun, partial shade in hot climates

Soil: rich, moist, pH 6.0 to 6.7

Water: medium to high

Range: Zones 4 to 9

Pests: powdery mildew

Remarks: native to the eastern United States, easy to grow

Marshall's Delight, with its vivid pink flowers and mildew resistance, is a proven selection.

Wild bee balm (*Monarda fistulosa*) comes in pink, lavender, and white and is often seen along roadsides and in wildflower gardens. It is more disease resistant and has more flavorful leaves than the hybrids.

Another species, *Monarda citriodora*, is a native herb prized for its leaves that smell like a cross between mint and camphor. Although this herb is called lemon mint, the foliage does not have a lemon scent. Its flowers are deep pink with purple spots.

Harvest, Storage, and Use

Harvest bee balm anytime in summer or fall. It blooms from July to September. Use the sweet-tasting flowers as a garnish for salads or desserts. Substitute the aromatic leaves for mint, dry them for tea, or add them to regular tea to give a hint of flavor. Bee balm is excellent for cut flowers, and its leaves can be used fresh in wreaths. You can also dry leaves and flowers to use in sachets and potpourris. For drying, pick just before flowers open or when they are in the seedpod stage.

Troubleshooting

Some hybrid selections of bee balm are susceptible to powdery mildew. To prevent mildew, choose disease-resistant selections and thin out clumps to allow for plenty of air circulation. Remove diseased plants promptly and do a thorough garden cleanup in fall.

HERBS THAT ATTRACT BEES AND HUMMINGBIRDS

These herbs need full sun and will attract a host of flying creatures to your garden, including many butterflies as well as bees and hummingbirds.

basil	marjoram
bee balm	Mexican bush
borage	sage
catnip	Mexican mint
chives	marigold
fennel	mint
germander	oregano
hyssop	ornamental
lavender	salvia
lemon balm	pineapple sage
	thyme

Bee balm adds vibrant color and a spicy aroma to your garden.

Borage

The nodding flowers of borage are popular as a garnish.

Borage is a fast-growing summer annual that produces large, gray-green leaves known for their cool, cucumber-like flavor. Originally from the Middle East, this herb lends an exotic feel to the garden. In midsummer, it bears nodding, star-shaped blooms that attract a host of bees, which explains its old-fashioned name, bee bread. When the edible flowers bloom, they are a striking periwinkle blue and then fade to light pink. The blooms make a colorful addition to punches and desserts and are often crystallized in sugar.

In the Landscape

Growing 1 to 3 feet tall, borage is useful as an ornamental. Plant it in the middle or back of an herb bed or flower border, as it will stretch to 3 feet when it sends up its bloom stalk. Borage has long, basal leaves and should have plenty of room. Contrast its blue blossoms with other flowering herbs, such as pink bee balm or white feverfew, or plant borage in containers.

Planting and Care

Borage is best grown from seed in full sun. It will reseed year after year (sometimes producing a second set of plants in the same growing season). Sow seeds in the spring after danger of frost is past. Keep the ground moist while seeds are germinating. When seedlings are 3 inches high, thin them to 6 inches apart.

Plant borage in soil that is average and well drained, with a pH of 6.0 to 7.0; the herb grows best if the soil has been tilled. Add a slow-release fertilizer to the soil before or during planting, and feed the plants with a balanced liquid fertilizer after heavy harvesting.

Species and Selections

The creeping selection (*Borago laxiflora*), a native of Corsica, is a good choice for rock gardens. For white-flowered borage, try Alba (*Borago officinalis* Alba), which is imported from England.

AT A GLANCE
❖
BORAGE
Borago officinalis

Features: sprawling summer plant with edible leaves and flowers

Uses: culinary, landscaping

Type: annual

Height: 1 to 3 feet

Width: 1 to 1½ feet

Light: full sun

Soil: average, well drained, pH 6.0 to 7.0

Water: medium

Range: Zones 3 to 10

Pests: none specific

Remarks: reseeds easily

Harvest, Storage, and Use

Harvest only young leaves and flowers, as the leaves of borage become woolly and tough with age. Because the hairy older leaves can irritate sensitive skin, you may want to use gloves when working around the plants.

Fresh borage wilts, so use young leaves quickly or dry them for future use. Finely chop fresh leaves (to improve their texture), and use them in salads in place of cucumbers, in sandwiches, cream cheese, yogurt, and dips. Add flowers as a last-minute garnish to spinach salads, to beverages, and to desserts. Or take a tip from the Romans—float borage blossoms in your wine.

Try dried borage leaves in herb teas.

CRYSTALLIZED BORAGE BLOSSOMS

To crystallize borage blossoms for use on cakes and other desserts, dip the flowers into whipped egg whites, and then into sugar; allow to dry. Store in a tightly sealed container.

Borage likes full sun and plenty of room.

Burnet

Burnet grows in a mounding form that can reach 1 foot in height.

In the morning, the lacy fernlike leaves of burnet glitter with dew, adding a sparkle to the herb garden. Young leaves, which have a mild cucumber taste, are perfect in salads or cool drinks. Most often called salad burnet, this is a short-lived hardy perennial that may become one of your favorite herbs.

In the Landscape

Burnet grows as rosettes of foliage that may reach as much as 3 feet in height. It is evergreen through the winter and can make a striking specimen plant. Use it as a green backdrop for colorful spring or fall annuals, such as pansies or marigolds. Because it forms a large, neat, circular mound, do not plant burnet too close to other plants where it can become buried by competing foliage.

Planting and Care

Plant burnet in morning sun or partial shade, shielding it from the hot summer sun. Start from seed in spring or fall. It is best to sow burnet directly in the garden rather than start it from transplants. If you choose to use transplants, select young plants, as the plant develops a deep root as it matures.

Sow seeds just below the surface of the soil and cover them lightly, but do not bury them. The seeds should germinate in about ten days. When the seedlings are 2 to 3 inches tall, thin them to 12 to 15 inches apart.

Burnet likes average soil with a pH of 6.0 to 6.8; if the soil is too rich or moist, the rosettes will rot. Fertilize the soil with a slow-release fertilizer before planting and then again the following spring. In the South, burnet performs well when mulched year-round.

The flowers bloom in the spring of the second year. They are reddish pink, growing on wiry stems that give the plant a ragged look. To keep plants tidy and to encourage a constant supply of tender young leaves, clip the flower stalks as they appear and harvest the leaves regularly. Although burnet is perennial, the leaves become bitter after it flowers; for the best flavor, replant every second or third year or let burnet flower and reseed. Then thin the seedlings to the recommended spacing and uproot the old plants.

Harvest, Storage, and Use

To harvest burnet, simply pick the leaves as needed, clipping an entire stem at a time. Leaves taste best in fall and early spring, and the young leaves are more tender and flavorful than the old ones. Because burnet is evergreen, fresh leaves are available year-round. This herb does not dry well but may be chopped and frozen or preserved in vinegar. (See page 38 for instructions for making herb vinegars.) Enjoy burnet fresh, but harvest at the last minute as it wilts quickly. Use burnet liberally as a garnish in place of parsley, or add burnet leaves to white wine or cool summer drinks. Let it flavor salads, sandwiches, cheese spreads, and sauces. Combine it with parsley, rosemary, or tarragon.

Troubleshooting

The rosettes of burnet are especially vulnerable to rot in Florida and the deep South where the winters are mild and the summers are humid. See page 125 for more information about rot.

BURNET FINGER SANDWICHES

4 slices whole wheat bread
2 tablespoons butter or margarine, softened
2 tablespoons cream cheese, softened
1 teaspoon minced fresh burnet

Remove crusts from bread. Spread one side of each slice with butter; spread cream cheese on top of butter. Sprinkle burnet evenly over cream cheese; top with remaining slices of bread. Cut into finger sandwiches. Yield: 6 finger sandwiches.

The scalloped leaves of burnet have a mild cucumber-like taste.

Catnip

Catnip produces small white flowers; pinch plants back to produce more foliage.

Catnip is a mintlike herb that will reward you with a good summer ground cover. Growing 1 to 3 feet tall, this hardy perennial spreads easily, which is a bonus if you like to drink catnip tea or make catnip sachets for gifts. However, most gardeners grow catnip for their cats, delighting as they watch their pets rub against the foliage.

In the Landscape

Catnip has coarse, gray-green leaves and a shrublike form. It prefers a spot of its own, such as a rock garden or wildflower garden, where it can spread with abandon. In a flower garden, catnip foliage provides a good backdrop for summer perennial flowers, such as purple coneflower. It can be planted with catmint (a member of the same genus), which has attractive blue flowers in summer. Catnip may take a beating from cats rubbing up against it, so plant it away from any treasured herbs. You can also grow catnip in containers.

Planting and Care

Start catnip from transplants or from seed sown in spring or fall. Sow seeds in average, well-drained soil with a pH of 6.6. When seedlings are 2 to 3 inches tall, thin them to 12 to 18 inches apart. Or you can set out divisions in the spring, or root stem cuttings in the summer.

Small white flowers appearing in mid- to late summer will attract bees. If you grow catnip for its foliage, pinch buds back to ensure abundant new growth.

Catnip reseeds and spreads quickly, so be prepared to pull seedlings and dig shoots that spread too far.

AT A GLANCE

❖

CATNIP
Nepeta cataria

Features: aromatic, minty herb; foliage attractive to cats

Uses: crafts, culinary, landscaping

Type: perennial

Height: 1 to 3 feet

Width: 1½ feet, but may spread

Light: full sun to partial shade

Soil: average, well drained, pH 6.6

Water: medium

Range: Zones 4 to 8

Pests: none specific

Remarks: spreads easily, keep seedlings under control

Species and Selections

There are several different types of catnip. The most common is *Nepeta cataria;* try the lemon-scented selection, Citriodora.

Do not confuse common catnip with Persian catnip *(Nepeta mussinii),* also called catmint. This is a more attractive plant for landscaping but is not a magnet for cats. It grows about 1 foot tall with long stalks full of periwinkle blooms in summer.

Harvest, Storage, and Use

Harvest catnip throughout the growing season. You can enjoy it fresh or dried. Air-drying helps it keep its minty scent. Common catnip has long been valued as the main ingredient in a soothing tea.

Enclose dried catnip (both leaves and blossoms) in cloth sachets and place in cat beds. Or make a mouse-shaped sachet of dried catnip, and give it, along with a potted catnip seedling, to a cat-loving friend. For a sachet that requires no sewing, simply stuff a tiny sock with catnip.

SOOTHING CATNIP TEA

2 cups water
2 tablespoons fresh catnip leaves
2 tablespoons fresh spearmint leaves
Honey (optional)

Boil water; add catnip and spearmint leaves. Cover and remove from heat; let stand at least 10 minutes until water acquires a minty flavor. Pour mixture through a wire-mesh strainer and discard leaves. Add honey to sweeten, if desired. For stronger tea, chop leaves first or add more leaves to taste. Yield: 2 cups.

A mouse-shaped sachet filled with catnip is a welcomed gift for friends with cats.

Chives

Chives boast pretty lavender blooms in spring, making them attractive herbs for flower beds as well as herb gardens.

Chives are hardy perennials that are attractive, tasty, and easy to grow. These rugged herbs grow in lush grasslike clumps that rise from a cluster of small bulbs. The snipped leaves add a pleasing touch to soups, salads, and vegetable dishes, providing both color and a mild onion or garlic flavor. In spring and summer, chives boast globelike flowers that are popular as edible garnishes.

In the Landscape

Use chives as a perennial edging or border plant in a flower bed or herb garden. Depending on the selection, chives grow 10 to 20 inches tall and have the same tidy appearance as ornamental liriope. In late spring and summer, lavender and white blooms will add fresh color to your garden. Chives also grow well in containers.

Planting and Care

Plant chives in full sun; plants will survive in partial shade, but the mounds will not be as full.

For quickest results, start with purchased plants or transplants and set them out in the garden in early spring. In the lower and Gulf South, plant chives in fall for a winter harvest.

You can also grow chives from seed, but it will take a year to produce a clump large enough to use. Sow seeds directly in the garden after the last frost. When seedlings are about 3 inches tall, thin them to 8 inches apart. (See page 32 for instructions on how to start seed indoors.)

Chives like rich, well-drained soil with a pH of 6.0 to 7.0. Add a slow-release fertilizer to the soil before or during planting. Keep faded blooms pinched back to promote leaf growth. If you harvest often, fertilize plants every two weeks with a balanced liquid fertilizer diluted according to label directions. About every three to four years, divide the clumps in early spring or after flowering, as the bulbs can become too crowded.

Species and Selections

Common chives *(Allium schoenoprasum)* have hollow leaves with a mild onion flavor. Plants grow to 10 to 12 inches tall. The leaves disappear in the fall at first freeze and reappear in early spring. Soon after, the plants produce lavender flowers that can be used to make a rose-colored vinegar. The selection Profusion has long-lasting edible flowers that do not form seeds.

AT A GLANCE
❖
CHIVES
Allium species

Features: grasslike herb with onion-flavored leaves and flowers

Uses: culinary, landscaping

Type: perennial

Height: 10 to 20 inches

Width: 8 to 16 inches

Light: full sun

Soil: rich, well drained, pH 6.0 to 7.0

Water: medium

Range: Zones 4 to 10

Pests: none specific

Remarks: prolific reseeders, divide every 3 or 4 years

Garlic chives grow taller than common chives, have garlic-flavored leaves, and bear white blooms in late summer.

Garlic chives *(Allium tuberosum)* are also called Chinese chives. They grow about twice as large as common chives and feature flatter, wider leaves. Garlic chives have a mild garlic flavor and are popular in Asian cooking. They are also appreciated in flower beds, where they grow to 20 inches tall when in bloom. Their white *umbel* of flowers, the flat or rounded flower cluster that springs from the same point, appears in mid- to late summer when many other perennials have begun to fade. Garlic chives are evergreen in areas where winters are mild. If the flowers are left to go to seed, many seedlings will sprout the next spring.

Harvest, Storage, and Use

Harvest chives as you need them. In the Gulf South, it is especially important to harvest often to encourage new growth. Rather than shearing the entire plant, select leaves from the outside of the clump and cut each one about ½ inch above soil level. Cutting them higher may leave unsightly brown stubs.

If you have more chives than you can use at the moment, chop fresh leaves and freeze them in water in ice cube trays. Infuse oils with fresh chives or preserve the herbs in butters and vinegars.

Add chives to dishes at the end of the cooking process, as their mild flavor can be destroyed by heat. Chives are excellent in egg dishes, potatoes, sauces, and with vegetables. Garnish cold soups and salads, including garden, pasta, and potato salads, with the leaves and blooms of garlic chives.

Troubleshooting

When harvesting chives, do not cut down the entire clump because the plant needs some of its leaves to ensure future growth.

CHICKEN KIEV

¼ cup plus 2 tablespoons butter, softened
1 teaspoon minced fresh parsley
1 small clove garlic, minced
1 tablespoon chopped fresh chives
¼ teaspoon salt
⅛ teaspoon ground white pepper
6 chicken breast halves, skinned and boned
1 egg, beaten
1 tablespoon water
½ cup all-purpose flour
1½ to 2 cups soft breadcrumbs
Vegetable oil

Combine first 6 ingredients in a small bowl; stir until blended. Shape butter mixture into a 3-inch stick; cover and freeze about 45 minutes or until firm.

Place chicken breast halves between 2 sheets of wax paper. Flatten to ¼-inch thickness, using a meat mallet or rolling pin.

Cut herb butter into 6 pats; place 1 pat in center of each chicken breast. Fold long sides of breast over butter; fold ends over, and secure with wooden picks.

Combine egg and water, beating well. Dredge each piece of chicken in flour; dip in egg mixture, and dredge in breadcrumbs.

Pour oil to depth of 2 to 3 inches in a Dutch oven; heat to 350°. Fry chicken 4 to 5 minutes or until done. Drain well. Yield: 6 servings.

Cilantro

Cilantro, also known as Chinese parsley, is grown both for its spicy-flavored foliage and for its seeds.

Leafy green cilantro is really two herbs in one. Its aromatic seeds, called coriander, are used in candy and pastries. Its tangy foliage, known as cilantro (or Chinese parsley), is a staple in Spanish, Asian, and other international cuisines. Surprisingly, the flavor of the seeds differs from the flavor of the foliage. Coriander seeds are fragrant while cilantro leaves are pungent.

In the Landscape

Cilantro is a cool-weather annual that grows 2 to 3 feet tall in spring or fall. A delicate plant with lacy leaves, it bears white or pinkish blossoms when the weather gets warm. Use cilantro as a back-of-the-border plant, or plant it in a bed devoted to annuals, such as dill, where it can reseed.

Planting and Care

Grow cilantro in full sun and well-drained soil with a pH of 6.6; it will tolerate light shade in the lower South.

Fall is the best time to plant cilantro in Zones 8, 9, and 10, where it rarely freezes enough to kill the plant. Cilantro seedlings are evergreen in winter throughout most of the South. If you live north of Zone 6, plant it in the spring after danger of frost is past.

Because it has delicate roots, cilantro is difficult to transplant. For best results, plant it during cool, moist weather. It is best to sow the seeds where they are to grow. Keep the seeds moist until germination. When the seedlings are 3 inches tall, you will need to thin them to 10 inches apart.

Once the plant blooms, foliage becomes scarce, so for a steady supply of fresh foliage, make successive sowings every three to four weeks through fall. Fertilize with a balanced liquid fertilizer after heavy harvesting.

The flowers eventually turn into light brown fruit with an edible inner seed. While the fresh seeds and foliage have a pungent odor, the ripe seeds become more fragrant as they dry. Cilantro reseeds and returns the following year.

Species and Selections

There are several different selections of this herb, some better for foliage than for seeds. The selections Slow-Bolting and Long Standing resist going to seed and produce a good crop of leaves over a long period.

AT A GLANCE

❖

CILANTRO (CORIANDER)
Coriandrum sativum

Features: pungent leaves with flavorful seedheads

Uses: crafts, culinary, landscaping

Type: annual

Height: 2 to 3 feet

Width: 1 foot

Light: full sun to light shade

Soil: rich, well drained, pH 6.6

Water: medium

Range: Zones 4 to 10

Pests: aphids, mildew, whiteflies, wilt

Remarks: has strong flavor

Harvest, Storage, and Use

You can harvest cilantro's foliage continually in the cooler months of spring and fall and through winter in the lower and Gulf South. The larger lower leaves are less pungent than the fernlike upper leaves. Be careful not to cut more than one-third of the leaves at a time, or you may weaken the plant.

Use chopped fresh foliage in black beans, salsas, stir-fries, and Mexican dishes. You may want to use the carrotlike root in Asian dishes as it has a more intense flavor than the leaves. Add leaves at the last minute for maximum seasoning, but remember that cilantro easily dominates, so use it sparingly. It marries well with chives, cumin, garlic, marjoram, mint, and peppers. Use the fragrant flowers in floral or herb arrangements. To preserve cilantro leaves for future use, freeze them in water or oil; they lose most of their flavor when dried.

Harvest the seedheads as soon as they ripen, or the weak stems will bend and the seeds will drop. (If you want cilantro to self-sow for next year's crop, leave a few seedheads standing in the garden.) Clip the seedhead halfway down the stem, and place it in a paper bag or basket. Put the bag in a well-ventilated spot. In five to six days, the dry husks will split into two halves, allowing the seeds inside to fall out.

Store coriander seeds in the refrigerator. Add a dash to sautéed fresh mushrooms, or use in relishes, pickles, or Indian dishes.

Troubleshooting

Cilantro occasionally has problems with aphids, mildew, whiteflies, and wilt. To prevent or control mildew and wilt, remove spent cilantro plants at the end of the season. See pages 124-125 for more information about these pests and diseases.

FRESH SALSA

1 small purple onion, quartered
2 jalapeño peppers, seeded and quartered
2 cloves garlic
¼ cup chopped fresh cilantro
2 tablespoons fresh lime juice
1 teaspoon salt
1 (14½-ounce) can diced tomatoes, drained

Position knife blade in food processor bowl; add first 6 ingredients. Pulse six times or until finely chopped.

Combine onion mixture and tomatoes in a small bowl, stirring well. Cover and store in refrigerator up to one week. Yield: 2 cups.

Cilantro produces fruit clusters that contain the edible seeds known as coriander.

Dill

Dill grows tall, lanky stems and fine graceful foliage that peaks in spring.

Dill is an annual herb whose fragrant, delicate-tasting leaves, also known as dillweed, will enhance a variety of your favorite foods. Yet dill brings as much to the landscape as it does to the palate. Its finely textured blue-green foliage grows on upright stalks of fountainous stems. In late spring, you may want to cut dill's chartreuse flowers and use them in a flower arrangement. Dill also produces pungent seeds that you can easily dry and store for culinary use, particularly for dill pickles. After seeds are set, dill plants will die, but you can sow the seed again in late summer and early fall.

In the Landscape

Dill is a cool-weather annual that grows in spring and fall. Plants reach 2 to 3 feet tall with graceful leaves branching from hollow stems. Yellowish green flowers borne in flat umbels electrify the garden in spring and fall. Use dill in the middle or back of a border, and plant it where it can be allowed to reseed. Dill can be grouped with other cool-weather annuals and biennials, such as cilantro and parsley.

Planting and Care

Plant dill in full sun. Choose a place where the stalks are protected from strong winds, or be prepared to stake the plants. Dill likes rich, well-drained soil with a pH of 5.5 to 6.5. Enrich the soil with organic matter before planting, and add a slow-release fertilizer to the soil before or during planting.

In spring, sow seeds two to four weeks before the last frost; in fall, sow again about two months before frost. For a continuous supply of foliage, make successive sowings every two weeks in spring until seeds stop germinating in the heat of summer. Water when the weather is dry.

It is best to sow the seeds directly in the garden. Plant them in rows, or spread them over the surface of the planting site and cover with ¼ inch of soil. The seeds will sprout in 10 to 14 days. When the plants are 2 to 3 inches tall, thin them to 6 to 12 inches apart.

Because dill has a long, carrotlike root, starting it from transplants can be a challenge. Transplants tend to go to seed quickly without producing much foliage. If you start with transplants, choose small plants that are 2 to 3 inches tall.

When dill flowers in late spring, it is time to harvest the entire plant. If dill is planted in fall, it will be killed by the first frost. But if allowed to go to seed, it should sprout again from the fallen seed the

AT A GLANCE

❖

DILL
Anethum graveolens

Features: fragrant foliage with chartreuse flowers

Uses: culinary, landscaping

Type: annual

Height: 2 to 3 feet

Width: 1 foot

Light: full sun

Soil: rich, well drained, pH 5.5 to 6.5

Water: medium

Range: Zones 3 to 10

Pests: none specific

Remarks: self-sows readily, seedlings will reappear for many years following spring. Because dill self-sows readily, you may want to leave a few seedheads in the garden to begin next year's crop.

Do not plant dill near fennel; the two herbs can cross-pollinate with unpredictable results. Dill attracts the parsleyworm caterpillar, which grows into the black swallowtail butterfly. Gardeners often leave the caterpillars alone and plant extra dill to encourage these butterflies to come to their gardens.

Species and Selections

Most dill plants are tall and leggy, but the selection Dill Bouquet (*Anethum graveolens* Dill Bouquet) is shorter and more compact than common dill. It reaches only 2 feet in height and does not need staking. The foliage is also fuller and more plentiful. Dill Bouquet is excellent for growing in containers. Hedger is a European selection ideal for cut flowers as it produces few seeds and is suitable for cutting over a long time.

Harvest, Storage, and Use

You can harvest dill foliage anytime from seedling stage until the plants bloom. When the plant begins to flower and set seed, harvest the entire plant and preserve the foliage. Use the flowers in arrangements.

Dill's flowers appear two or three months after planting. Pinch the blooms to encourage more foliage.

To harvest dill seeds, collect them when they first turn brown, or they will soon drop off. Cut the seedhead halfway down the stalk, and hang it upside down in a paper bag in a dry, well-ventilated place. After the seeds drop into the bag, store them in an airtight container. Dill's pungent seeds can be used in pickles, breads, salad dressings, and sauerkraut.

Dill leaves are best enjoyed fresh but can be frozen in water or stock, dried, or, if refrigerated, stored in butter or oil. Finely chop fresh dill for maximum flavor. Use it on fish, in beans, eggs, soups, sandwiches, vegetables (potatoes, cabbage, green beans), green salads, potato salads, sauces, and cheese. Dill makes a good salt substitute. Dried leaves tend to lose flavor in the drying process, so use them liberally.

DILLED SHRIMP

2 pounds unpeeled large fresh shrimp
½ cup butter or margarine
⅓ cup chopped green onions
2 large cloves garlic, crushed
1 tablespoon lemon juice
1 tablespoon chopped fresh dill
1 (2-ounce) jar diced pimiento, drained
3 cups cooked medium egg noodles
2 tablespoons butter or margarine
Salt and pepper to taste
Garnish: fresh dill sprigs

Peel and devein shrimp; set aside.

Combine ½ cup butter, green onions, and garlic in a 13- x 9- x 2-inch baking dish. Cover with heavy-duty plastic wrap, folding back a small section of wrap to allow steam to escape. Microwave at HIGH for 1 to 2 minutes or until butter melts and green onions are tender. Add shrimp and lemon juice, stirring to coat. Cover and microwave at HIGH for 4 minutes, stirring after 2 minutes. Stir in chopped dill. Cover and microwave at HIGH for 1 to 3 minutes or until shrimp turn pink. Let stand, covered, 1 minute. Stir in pimiento.

Combine hot cooked egg noodles, 2 tablespoons butter, salt, and pepper; stir until butter melts. Arrange seasoned noodles on a serving platter. Top with shrimp mixture. Garnish, if desired. Yield: 6 servings.

Edible Flowers

Marigolds brighten a salad garden while their blooms add a spicy, tarragon-like flavor to foods.

While not considered herbs, several well-known flowers yield colorful blossoms that can be eaten. Marigolds, nasturtiums, pansies, and roses are among those plants that can add a touch of color to your herb garden and turn simple salads into works of art. Try nestling a few yellow French marigold petals among sliced red tomatoes. Or toss bright orange nasturtiums and blue pansies into a mix of spring salad greens. Edible flowers also make lovely garnishes for desserts and beverages, and rose petals are a favorite ingredient in teas, jellies, and potpourris.

Marigold

Popular annuals for late spring, summer, and fall color, marigolds grow from 6 to 20 inches tall, depending upon the selection. Their fernlike foliage and yellow and orange blooms make sunny borders. They are excellent container plants for adding color to the herb garden. Pair them with culinary herbs, such as basil or lemon verbena.

Marigolds like full sun and can be started from seed indoors or as purchased transplants. For best results, set out transplants in the spring after threat of frost is past. Young transplants do best, as older ones are often stunted, growing poorly after planting.

These flowers need fertile, well-drained soil with a pH of 6.0 to 7.0. Work a slow-release fertilizer into the soil before or during planting. Marigolds are moderately drought resistant but will need water during dry periods. Harvest blossoms regularly for garnishes and cut flowers; this will help the plants continue to flower.

Spider mites or heat stress can be a problem in the dead of summer. To discourage spider mites, periodically spray the underside of foliage. If plants start looking peaked, you can cut them back to encourage new growth; follow shearing with a feeding of balanced liquid fertilizer. Or set out new transplants in late summer.

For proven selections, try Signet type marigolds such as Lemon Gem (yellow) or Tangerine Gem (orange). Dwarf selections, such as Dwarf French, thrive in containers or at the front of a border. Marigold combines well with spicy, floral flavors. Use the flowers as garnishes for pasta and salads. Or finely chop marigolds and add small portions to egg, cheese, and vegetable dishes.

AT A GLANCE

❖

MARIGOLD
Tagetes hybrids

Features: orange or yellow carnation-like flowers with spicy flavor

Uses: culinary, landscaping

Type: annual

Height: 6 to 20 inches

Width: 8 to 12 inches

Light: full sun

Soil: rich, well drained, pH 6.0 to 7.0

Water: medium

Range: Zones 3 to 9

Pests: spider mites

Remarks: grows best in spring and fall

The leaves and flowers of nasturtiums lend a peppery flavor to salads and sandwich spreads.

Nasturtium

Fast-growing nasturtiums produce luminous orange, yellow, or red flowers in the late spring, summer, and fall before succumbing to frost. They grow to 1 foot tall and 2 feet wide, with some climbing types stretching to 6 feet.

Natives of Peru, nasturtiums like full sun, but they suffer from the midsummer heat in Zone 7 and farther south. In these areas, plant them where they will receive four to six hours of sun, preferably morning sun and afternoon shade.

Nasturtiums grow in average, well-drained soil, with a pH of 6.0 to 8.0. Thin seedlings to 4 to 10 inches apart. Do not plant these annuals in rich soil. They will produce more flowers in poor soil. In rich, moist soil, plants produce foliage but few flowers.

Transplants are rarely available; therefore, nasturtiums are typically grown from seed. Sow seeds outdoors in late winter or early spring as soon as the soil warms in order to get plants up and in shape to survive the summer. Soak seeds overnight to speed germination by as much as a week. Sow seeds ½ to 1 inch deep and 1½ to 3 inches apart. Save some seeds, and if plants die in the heat of July, plant more nasturtiums at the beginning of August for fall flowers. Be sure to water regularly as with any August planting.

For named selections, try Jewel Mixed. If you want nasturtiums to plant in containers, look for dwarf selections.

To use nasturtium foliage, pick the young growth at the stem tips. The large, blue-green leaves have a peppery flavor similar to watercress and can be used in salads and sandwiches. The foliage is also lovely in fresh herb and flower arrangements. Harvest flowers at any stage. The fragrant red and orange flowers are hot and peppery like radishes. Use them as garnishes, or shred them and add to salads, cold vegetables, or pesto dishes.

Nasturtiums can be bothered by aphids and leaf diseases. To prevent leaf spot, space plants far apart, and avoid watering early in the morning before the dew dries. Remove any affected plants as soon as possible.

AT A GLANCE

❖

NASTURTIUM
Tropaeolum majus

Features: orange, yellow, or red cottage flowers with watercress flavor

Uses: culinary, landscaping

Type: annual

Height: 1 to 6 feet

Width: 2 feet

Light: full sun

Soil: average, well drained pH 6.0 to 8.0

Water: medium

Range: Zones 3 to 9

Pests: aphids, leaf diseases

Remarks: good flowering ground cover or climber

Harvest pansy blooms for a colorful garnish.

AT A GLANCE

PANSY
Viola x *Wittrockiana*

Features: colorful, old-fashioned bedding plant with edible blooms

Uses: culinary, landscaping

Type: annual

Height: 4 to 12 inches

Width: 6 to 10 inches

Light: full sun

Soil: rich, well drained, pH 6.0 to 7.0

Water: medium

Range: Zones 4 to 8

Pests: none specific

Remarks: cut back leggy plants for compact new growth and more flowers

Pansy

Pansies are low-growing annuals that yield fall, winter, and spring color. They reach 4 to 12 inches tall and come in a variety of colors, from muted pastels to bright yellows, blues, whites, and deep mauves. They are ideal for mixing with culinary herbs, such as chives, parsley, or winter savory, in containers.

The easiest way to grow pansies is from transplants. Plant them in full sun in spring or fall. Fall plantings do best in the South; the plants grow roots during winter and reach twice the size and produce more flowers than those planted the following spring.

Pansies need rich, well-drained soil with a pH of 6.0 to 7.0. Work in a slow-release fertilizer before or during planting. Set transplants 6 to 8 inches apart. Water until well established; thereafter, water one inch per week. Pansies will flower more abundantly with periodic feedings of a liquid fertilizer that is high in phosphorus, such as 15-30-15.

You can snip pansy blooms from the plants as they appear. The blooms have a mild, slightly fruity flavor and make excellent garnishes for salads, ice cream, or fresh fruit dishes. For selections, try large-blooming types such as Swiss Giant or Majestic Giant; medium-sized flowers such as Crown, Joker, or Roc; or small multiflora pansies such as Maxim or Crystal Bowl.

Rose

Roses have been companions of herbs for centuries, adding color, structure, and fragrance to the garden. Their petals have long been used in teas, jellies, rose water, and potpourris.

The best roses for culinary use are old-fashioned or species roses (such as *Rosa rugosa)* that do not have to be sprayed for diseases and pests (unlike the more finicky hybrids). These roses are also more fragrant than modern roses. Some old-fashioned roses can grow rather large,

ROSE AND LEMON TEA

2 quarts water

½ cup finely crushed lemon verbena

2 tablespoons chamomile flowers (or 1 small chamomile tea bag)

2 tablespoons whole rosebuds

1 tablespoon whole rosemary leaves

Boil water; stir in remaining ingredients. Cover, remove from heat, and steep 20 minutes. Pour mixture through a wire-mesh strainer, and discard leaves. Yield: 2 quarts.

however; consider selections, such as Fairy, that maintain a manageable size of 3 feet by 3 feet and bloom continuously. Otherwise, be prepared to prune. In the herb garden, shrub roses make excellent hedges, specimens, or back-of-the border plants along a fencerow.

Roses must have full sun. Plant them in fall or spring in rich, well-drained soil with a pH of 6.0 to 7.0. Amend soil with compost or other organic matter. Fertilize with slow-release rose fertilizer before planting and again in midsummer. Mulch roses to keep roots moist, but do not let the mulch reach the crown of the plants. Keep flowers cut to prolong blooming.

These plants are susceptible to a host of diseases and insects. These include aphids, powdery mildew, spider mites, whiteflies, and black spot, a fungus disease peculiar only to roses that causes black spots and yellowing of leaves. The more hot and humid the climate, the more pests there will be. But old roses are much more tolerant of these pests than modern roses and usually will not succumb to them. See pages 124-125 for more information about these pests and diseases.

To reduce the chance of disease, water roses at the base of the plant with a hose or drip irrigation system. This is better than an overhead sprinkler, which wets foliage and splashes soil on the plant. Give roses a 1-inch soaking this way once a week. Prune back dead branches.

Rose petals have a delicate flavor and can be added to teas, wines, sweet dishes, desserts, and sugars. (See page 36 for details on making herb sugars.) For craft purposes, harvest newly opened roses on a dry morning. Dry a few rosebuds, too, for finishing touches. Air-dry buds and petals. Make sure petals are completely dry before using, or they will mold.

Harvest, Storage, and Use

Harvest flowers of marigolds, nasturtiums, pansies, and roses when they have just opened. Frequent harvesting will produce more flowers. Before using, soak flowers in cold water for a few minutes to get rid of any insects among the petals. Use flowers sparingly at first, adding more to taste. When including flowers in salads, use little dressing and add flowers last (after tossing the salad) as the vinegar or lemon in the dressing will discolor petals.

Avoid spraying with pesticides if you plan to eat the flowers, or use only products that are approved for food crops. If you have the slightest doubt about whether a flower in your garden is edible, call your local Extension agent.

Rose petals have a long history of use as a flavoring.

AT A GLANCE

❖

ROSE
Rosa species

Features: classic additions to the herb garden; aromatic, edible flowers

Uses: crafts, culinary, landscaping

Type: perennial

Height: 2 to 12 feet

Width: 3 to 8 feet

Light: full sun

Soil: rich, well drained, pH 6.0 to 7.0

Water: medium

Range: Zones 4 to 10

Pests: aphids, black spot, powdery mildew, spider mites, whiteflies

Remarks: choose disease-tolerant types

Fennel

Fennel flowers, which appear in summer, are also an edible part of the plant.

Fennel is a handsome Mediterranean plant whose distinctive flavor has traditionally been used to season seafood. Much valued by the Romans, it is one of the oldest cultivated plants. Today, thanks to its green or bronze foliage and impressive height, fennel is also valued as an ornamental. Nothing goes to waste when you grow fennel. In addition to the licorice-flavored foliage and seeds, you can eat the stems (like celery) and the sweet-tasting root.

In the Landscape

Sweet fennel is a hardy perennial that is evergreen in Zone 7 and farther south. Plants grow 1 to 5 feet tall, depending on the selection, and produce fine, fernlike foliage similar to that of dill. The glossy yellow-green or bronze leaves are borne on shiny green, hollow stems. In summer, fennel's yellow flowers are impressive, blooming in 6-inch umbels. Like dill, fennel's blooms attract beneficial insects. In a flower border, fennel foliage will provide a soft, complementary background for a broad range of flower and foliage colors. When in bloom, fennel becomes a tall accent plant. Pair bronze fennel with pink poppies, white daisies, or other spring-blooming perennials.

Planting and Care

Sweet fennel needs full sun but will benefit from partial shade in the afternoon. Start from transplants or seed. Sow seeds in spring after the last frost; seeds will germinate in about two weeks. When plants are 2 to 3 inches tall, thin to 8 to 12 inches apart. Fennel needs rich, well-drained soil with a pH of 6.0 to 6.7. Add a slow-release fertilizer to the soil before or during planting.

Fennel grows quickly, but in spite of its height, the plant rarely needs staking. After flowering, the plant may look messy, especially if you let the flowers set seed; cut the plant back to about a foot from the ground, and it will put out new growth. If you are growing fennel for foliage or for bulbs, it is best to keep flower heads pinched back so that they do not set seed;

Cut fennel back after it flowers to encourage new growth at the base of the plant.

AT A GLANCE

FENNEL
Foeniculum vulgare

Features: large, handsome herb with green or bronze foliage

Uses: crafts, culinary, landscaping

Type: perennial and annual

Height: 1 to 5 feet

Width: 1 to 2 feet

Light: full sun to partial shade

Soil: rich, well drained, pH 6.0 to 6.7

Water: medium

Range: Zones 6 to 9

Pests: aphids

Remarks: easily reseeds, all parts of the plant useful

pinching back promotes leaf growth and larger bulbs. However, you can encourage new plants if you let a few flowers set seed. Transplant seedlings that sprout early in spring when they are very small.

Fennel is tolerant of light frost and can be harvested for several months in cool weather. As the plant matures, it will return larger for the first three years.

Do not plant fennel near dill, as the two herbs can cross-pollinate with unpredictable results. Also, do not grow fennel near cilantro, as it can reduce fennel's seed production.

Species and Selections

Bronze fennel *(Foeniculum vulgare* Baloquese), a selection of sweet fennel, is treasured for its plumelike coppery leaves, which are denser than the leaves of the species. It is grown as an ornamental as well as an edible herb.

Florence fennel or finocchio *(Foeniculum Dulce)* is a dwarf annual selection grown for its thick bases, which overlap to form a false bulb that is eaten like a vegetable. Florence fennel grows 1 to 2 feet tall and is hardy in all but the coldest regions of the South. Along the Gulf Coast and in Florida, however, it may not grow well because of the mild winters.

Florence fennel requires a richer soil and more moisture than sweet fennel. The best way to start Florence fennel is from seeds, as the plants have a long taproot and do not transplant well. If you buy transplants, be sure that they are small. Thin seedlings to 6 to 8 inches apart. When the base is the size of an egg, you can mound soil around it to blanch it, which makes it milder in flavor and more tender. Harvest the bulb when it reaches 2½ to 3 inches in diameter. You can eat it raw or cooked. If you want to collect seeds, leave plants in the garden through winter; seed production occurs the second summer. Otherwise, harvest the entire plant.

Harvest, Storage, and Use

You can harvest the foliage, stems, and flowers of sweet fennel year-round. Use chopped leaves to garnish soups and salads. Put leaves in a bouquet garni to flavor fish dishes. Add leaves to seafood, tomato dishes, bean dishes, mayonnaise, vegetables, vinaigrettes, or butters for grilling fish. (See page 36 for details on making herb butters.) Use stems and flowers in salads to add a cool, sweet flavor.

From a distance, sweet fennel resembles dill; but fennel is taller and remains green through the winter in the lower South.

GRILLED FENNEL AND RADICCHIO

4 bulbs fennel
1 head radicchio, separated into leaves
½ cup orange juice
¼ cup orange marmalade
2 tablespoons olive oil
1 tablespoon white wine vinegar
2 cloves garlic, minced
½ teaspoon salt
¼ teaspoon freshly ground pepper
Vegetable cooking spray

Cut fennel bulbs vertically into ½-inch slices. Cook in boiling water to cover 3 minutes; drain. Combine fennel and radicchio in a large bowl; set aside.

Combine orange juice and next 6 ingredients in a jar. Cover tightly, and shake vigorously. Chill ¼ cup vinaigrette; pour remaining vinaigrette over fennel and radicchio, tossing to coat. Let fennel mixture stand 15 minutes; drain.

Coat grill rack with cooking spray; place on grill over medium-hot coals (350° to 400°). Place fennel on rack; cook, covered, 15 minutes, turning once. Add radicchio; cook, covered, 2 minutes. Toss fennel and radicchio with reserved vinaigrette. Yield: 4 servings.

Note: Do not core the fennel before grilling. The core will hold the slices of fennel together.

To store fennel, dry the foliage or freeze it in water. You can also make fennel vinegar or refrigerated oils to use later in marinades, sauces, and salad dressings. (See page 38 for information on how to make vinegars.)

Harvest the seeds when the stalks are dry and the umbels have turned brown but before the umbels shatter. Dry seeds by laying the flowers on paper for five to six days or until the seeds drop. (See page 40 for other methods of drying seeds.) Lightly crush the seeds to release their flavor, and sprinkle them into Italian sauces, pizzas, cabbage, pork, or sausage.

Troubleshooting

Fennel occasionally attracts a caterpillar known as the parsleyworm, which eventually turns into the black swallowtail butterfly. The best control is to leave a few extra fennel plants for the butterflies. Fennel may also be bothered by aphids. See page 124 for more information about this pest.

The fernlike stalks and yellow flowers of fennel tower above other herbs in this garden.

Feverfew

Feverfew blooms make excellent cut flowers. Double-flowered forms are especially popular for herb arrangements.

Feverfew is an ornamental perennial herb that enlivens a summer garden with its daisylike flowers. Once thought to relieve fevers, arthritis, and migraine headaches, feverfew is still studied for its curative effects, but you can grow it for its flowers. Dried feverfew flowers hold their color and form well, making them a good filler in floral arrangements.

In the Landscape

Feverfew may be planted in an herb garden, perennial border, or wildflower meadow. Its 1-inch-wide blossoms add refreshing color to the leafy green of an herb garden. When feverfew blooms in summer, its finely cut green leaves are obscured by clouds of tiny blossoms. If you trim the plant back slightly when the blooms fade, it will bloom again. At the end of the season, leave a few flowers if you want feverfew to self-sow, but be aware that it can spread quickly. Plant it where you need a mass of white or in an area where it can naturalize, and you can enjoy its flowers in midsummer and fall.

Planting and Care

This herb thrives in full sun or light shade. Plant seeds in the spring as soon as the soil can be worked, or set out transplants in spring or fall.

Give feverfew moderately fertile, well-drained soil with a pH of 6.0 to 6.7. Add a slow-release fertilizer before or during planting and fertilize again in spring; feed plants a second time with a balanced liquid fertilizer after shearing. To start your own transplants, propagate stem cuttings in late summer; cuttings will root in two to three weeks. Or start new plants from divisions made in spring or fall.

Species and Selections

Feverfew (*Chrysanthemum parthenium*) is also listed as *Tanacetum parthenium* in many sources. The single-flowering feverfew is the most common, growing 2 to 3 feet tall. White Pompon is a double-flowered selection that grows only 1 foot tall.

Harvest, Storage, and Use

Cut feverfew flowers when the plant begins to bloom; dry them to use in floral arrangements and other crafts. (See page 41 for more information.)

AT A GLANCE
❖
FEVERFEW
Chrysanthemum parthenium

Features: summer herb covered with white or yellow blooms

Uses: crafts, landscaping

Type: perennial

Height: 1 to 3 feet

Width: 1 to 2 feet

Light: full sun to partial shade

Soil: average, well drained, pH 6.0 to 6.7

Water: medium

Range: Zone 5 to 7

Pests: none specific

Remarks: reseeds easily, old-fashioned favorite

Garlic

Unlike leafy herbs, garlic is harvested from the soil. Refrigerate garlic oils and butters to ensure food safety.

A relative of the onion, garlic is easy to grow and does not require much space. It takes seven to nine months to produce a full-sized head of garlic, which is made up of 8 to 12 small cloves enclosed in a papery white skin. Once you begin to grow your own garlic, you will find that the different kinds, such as elephant and rocambole, offer flavors that make the wait worthwhile.

In the Landscape

A hardy perennial, garlic produces clumps of broad, flat, straplike leaves that grow 1 to 3 feet tall. It is usually planted in rows in a vegetable or herb bed but can be grown in groups to create a mass of striking vertical foliage in the garden or in a border. As the plants near harvest size, they send up a stalk with a large cluster of garlic-scented lavender flowers.

Planting and Care

Garlic requires a long, cool growing season. In the South, set cloves out in late summer or early fall to harvest the following spring or early summer. In the Gulf South, it is best to plant in October.

Always start garlic from cloves as they are easy to plant and will grow more quickly than seed. Garlic started from seed will take two years to produce cloves large enough to use. Plant garlic in rich, deep, well-drained soil. The herb is not sensitive to soil pH, growing in a wide range from 4.5 to 8.3. However, it is best to till and enrich the soil with organic matter. Add a slow-release fertilizer to the soil before or during planting and again each spring.

Space cloves 4 to 6 inches apart, with the pointed end up, and cover with 3 inches of soil. In late spring, clip off the flowers so the plant will produce a bulb.

If you plant garlic in early fall, the clove will produce roots and small shoots before the ground freezes. When the weather warms in the spring, the shoots will begin growing again. The cloves will multiply to form a cluster of cloves that make up a large head by midsummer. Dig up the head after the blooms die and the leaves turn yellow. Plant new cloves each year for highest production.

Species and Selections

Common softneck garlic *(Allium sativum)* is the easiest to grow and store. California selections, such as California Late White, are hardy and have a good shelf life. Inchelium Red is a flavorful, heavy producer.

AT A GLANCE
❖
GARLIC
Allium sativum

Features: tall herb with edible foliage, flowers, and bulbs
Uses: culinary, landscaping
Type: perennial
Height: 1 to 3 feet
Width: 1 foot
Light: full sun
Soil: rich, well drained, pH 4.5 to 8.3
Water: medium
Range: Zones 5 to 10
Pests: none specific
Remarks: essential culinary herb, plant in fall in the South

Giant garlic or elephant garlic *(Allium scorodoprasum)* has a milder flavor than true garlic and produces larger heads. An ancestor of the modern leek, giant garlic grows to 3 feet tall and produces cloves the size of small tulip bulbs, with five cloves to a head. Plant the cloves in late summer or fall. Place them 12 inches apart, with the pointed end up, and cover with 3 inches of soil. Clip flower stalks as they appear. Harvest giant garlic as you would true garlic. Separate the small cloves growing at the base of the bulb and plant them. These cloves will take two to three years to reach full size.

Rocambole garlic *(Allium sativum var. ophioscorodon)* is a milder, easy-to-peel form of common garlic. The favorite of many herb gardeners, it produces ribbonlike foliage that is excellent in salads.

Harvest, Storage, and Use

When the foliage has yellowed and withered, garlic is ready for harvest. If you are growing garlic as a perennial, harvest only three-fourths of the heads, leaving the remainder to multiply.

Dig garlic carefully, lifting heads from the ground to avoid injuring them. Store in a well-ventilated place out of direct sun for several days so that the skins will begin to dry. Then braid the stems and hang. Keep loose bulbs in net bags, or freeze individual cloves, peeled or unpeeled, in a plastic bag.

Garlic cloves enhance almost any dish and the mild-tasting leaves make a wonderful addition to salads. You can use the leaves until the heads are large enough to harvest. But be careful not to take more than one-third of the foliage from any one plant, or it will be weakened.

Braid common garlic, and hang it to dry out of the direct sun.

ROASTED GARLIC SPREAD

1 large head garlic, unpeeled
1 tablespoon olive oil
1 (8-ounce) package cream cheese, softened
¼ cup butter, softened
½ teaspoon salt
2 tablespoons minced fresh chives

Gently peel outer skin from garlic, leaving head intact. Place garlic in a small baking pan; drizzle with olive oil. Cover with aluminum foil, and bake at 350° for 25 minutes. Remove cover, and bake 8 to 10 additional minutes or until garlic is soft. Remove from oven, and cool completely. Remove and discard papery skin from garlic. Scoop out soft garlic pulp with a small spoon; set garlic pulp aside.

Beat cream cheese and butter at high speed with an electric mixer until fluffy. Add reserved garlic and salt; beat until blended. Stir in chives. Store spread in refrigerator; use promptly. Serve spread over warm slices of French bread.
Yield: 1¼ cups.

Note: Garlic oils and butters should be refrigerated immediately and used promptly.

Geranium, Scented

Valued for its sculptural form as well as its fragrant foliage, scented geranium is an excellent addition to container herb gardens.

Scented geranium is usually grown for its variety of strongly scented leaves, whose aromas resemble those of other plants. Apple, lemon, licorice, rose, and strawberry are a few scents found in this large collection of unusual South African natives. Scented geraniums are tender tropicals grown as annuals or container plants because they cannot withstand freezing temperatures. Their flowers are usually inconspicuous, but a few selections have colorful blooms large enough to be edible. Popular since Victorian times, scented geranium leaves add a charming surprise to cakes, herb butters, teas, and crafts.

Although scented geranium is grown for its leaves, a few types have showy blossoms.

In the Landscape

Plant scented geraniums where you can rub the leaves to release their scent. These plants are characterized by woody stems, unusual shapes, and irregular plant forms. Use them to add visual interest to your landscape.

Growing only 1 to 3 feet tall, scented geraniums are well suited for containers. Place a collection of these plants where you can enjoy their sweet perfume—near an entryway, on a set of steps, on a patio, or beside a walkway. Train scented geraniums as topiaries or hang a basket of these fragrant herbs at nose level. Plant two or three different kinds of scented geraniums in large containers for a living potpourri of scents. Scented geraniums do bloom, but the small white, red, or lavender flowers of most selections do not attract much attention.

Planting and Care

Start scented geraniums from purchased transplants or rooted tip cuttings taken anytime from spring to fall. Set the young plants outdoors in full sun to partial shade after threat of frost is past in late spring.

Morning sun is best in the lower South. If plants become leggy, move them to a brighter location. Shape plants by trimming awkward stems when blooming is finished. Use clippings in cooking or crafts.

Scented geraniums like rich, well-drained soil with a pH of 6.0 to 7.0. Add a slow-release fertilizer to the soil before or during planting. Once they bloom, feed them with a balanced liquid fertilizer. If you grow the plants in a container, be sure it drains well, as scented geraniums can drown if left sitting in water. Let the top of the soil dry out between waterings. Check regularly to make certain plants are not pot-bound; replant as needed. Like outdoor plants, those grown in containers prefer morning sun and filtered sunlight in the afternoon.

You can keep scented geraniums through winter by cutting plants back in early fall and bringing them indoors to overwinter. Place in a cool spot and water sparingly. Or root stem cuttings and overwinter those. (See page 32 for more on propagation.) Put potted geraniums in a sunny location or under lights for at least half a day. Keep plants clipped during the winter so that they do not get too leggy.

Species and Selections

There are many different selections of scented geraniums. Scents to choose from include apple, coconut, lemon, orange, peppermint, pine, rose, and strawberry. Leaves of some types are tiny and delicate, while leaves of others are large and rippled. For use in hanging baskets, try selections such as Sprawling Coconut paired with herbs such as prostrate rosemary and creeping thyme. Add trailing verbena and similar summer annuals for color.

Harvest, Storage, and Use

The foliage and flowers of scented geranium are edible. Scented leaves are used for flavoring cakes, herb butter, jelly, iced tea, and even barbecue sauce. If you do not want to cook with the foliage, cut stems for summer arrangements or collect and dry the leaves for potpourris; store in airtight containers. Or crush scented geranium and treat yourself to a handful of fragrance while working in the garden.

Troubleshooting

Scented geraniums are remarkably tough, but watch them for signs of insects. Aphids and whiteflies can be a problem, as well as can spider mites. See pages 124-125 for more information about these pests.

ROSE GERANIUM POUND CAKE

6 large rose geranium leaves
Vegetable cooking spray
¾ cup margarine, softened
3 cups sugar
8 egg whites
1½ cups buttermilk
2 teaspoons vanilla extract
4½ cups sifted cake flour
¾ teaspoon baking soda
¼ teaspoon baking powder
¼ teaspoon salt

Coat geranium leaves with cooking spray; arrange leaves, dull side up, in bottom of a 10-inch tube pan lined with wax paper and coated with cooking spray and flour. Set aside.

Beat margarine at medium speed with an electric mixer until creamy; gradually add sugar, beating well. Add egg whites; beat well.

Combine buttermilk and vanilla, stirring well. Combine cake flour and remaining 3 ingredients; add to margarine mixture alternately with buttermilk mixture, beginning and ending with flour mixture. Mix well after each addition. Spoon batter into tube pan. Bake at 325° for 1 hour and 35 minutes or until a wooden pick inserted in center comes out clean. Cool in pan 10 minutes. Remove cake from pan, and cool completely on a wire rack. Yield: 16 servings.

Germander

The small leaves and compact habit of germander make it a good substitute for dwarf edging boxwood.

Few evergreen herbs perform as well in a traditional herb garden as the Mediterranean native, germander. George Washington is said to have loved this plant because he could walk outdoors in February to find germander's glossy green leaves spangled with a coat of frost. Germander flowers from July to September, the small blooms growing among leaves on upright stems. If you are looking for a dark green plant that can be clipped back for a low hedge or knot garden, this low-growing perennial is the best choice.

In the Landscape

Germander makes an excellent hedge or edging plant because of its compact growth. Sometimes called "poor man's boxwood," germander provides neat edges and focal points in an herb garden without the expense of slower-growing boxwood. Along with other evergreen herbs such as lavender, rosemary, thyme, and winter savory, germander will help your herb garden remain green throughout winter. Clip it for a formal look in geometric arrangements, or leave it to grow into its naturally compact shape. You may also prune germander into a topiary and arrange it with a few other topiaries in pots, such as bay or rosemary, to create a distinctive container garden. In the humid Gulf South, it is better to grow germander in a container as it may struggle through rainy summer weather.

Planting and Care

Start germander from transplants, as it is very slow to grow from seeds. Plant in full sun to partial shade in spring as soon as the soil has warmed, or plant in fall. (It is best to grow container plants in full sun.) Germander likes average, well-drained, slightly acidic soil with a pH of 6.0 to 6.7. Add a slow-release fertilizer to the soil before or during planting, and fertilize again each spring. North of Zone 7, be sure to mulch germander in the fall for winter protection.

To keep germander as a formal hedge, prune in early spring and periodically trim through the end of July. This encourages it to branch and fill out nicely.

Germander can be propagated by cuttings and layering, but taking divisions of the crowns in the fall is much faster.

Species and Selections

There are two popular species of germander. The smaller one, *Teucrium chamaedrys,* is often called Washington's germander.

AT A GLANCE
❖
GERMANDER
Teucrium species

Features: old-fashioned evergreen with glossy leaves

Uses: crafts, landscaping

Type: perennial

Height: 1½ to 2 feet

Width: 1½ to 2 feet

Light: full sun to partial shade

Soil: average, well drained, pH 6.0 to 6.7

Water: medium

Range: Zones 5 to 9

Pests: none specific

Remarks: popular in Elizabethan-style knot gardens

Long-lived and very hardy, this upright plant grows to 1½ feet tall and just as wide, taking the form of a minishrub in Zone 7 and south where it is evergreen. In Zones 5 and 6, it dies to the ground in winter, but comes back in spring. It has small, toothed green leaves and tiny pink blooms that appear in midsummer. A dwarf form, which grows only half as tall, is suitable for small-scale gardens.

The larger species, *Teucrium lucidum*, grows to 2 feet tall and has greenish gray leaves and little, creamy white blooms.

Harvest, Storage, and Use

Germander was once used for medicinal purposes. Today it is grown primarily as a landscape plant, although some gardeners harvest the aromatic foliage in late summer for wreaths and other crafts.

Evergreen throughout the South, germander makes an excellent container plant.

Germander combines with gray santolina, red barberry, and lavender to form an intricate pattern for this knot garden.

Lavender

Individual stems of lavender look delicate but make quite a show when the entire plant blooms.

Lavender is among the most popular ornamental herbs used for landscaping. Bringing to mind an old English garden, lavender's flowers fill the air with perfume beginning in late spring or early summer. In the winter, the herb's silver-green foliage often keeps its color and fragrance. A native of the Mediterranean, lavender is grown commercially in France for perfumes and cosmetics. You can use it in gourmet cooking, sachets, floral arrangements, and potpourris.

In the Landscape

A shrubby perennial, lavender offers many species and selections, with foliage ranging from dark silver to gray green. They grow from 1 to 2½ feet tall, and sometimes equally wide, depending upon the selection, the length of the growing season, and severity of winter. The flowers, which release a sweet fragrance, bloom from June to August and range in color from deep purple to pink to white. Lavender can be clipped as a low hedge in a formal garden. It also makes a sweet-smelling border along a path. A single plant or small grouping is a striking accent in a rock or natural herb garden.

Lavender is also an excellent plant for containers; in fact, in the deep South, it often does better in containers than in the ground because of the increased drainage and air circulation.

Planting and Care

Start lavender from transplants, as it is difficult to grow from seed. Choose an open location in full sun with good air circulation; lavender cannot tolerate excessive soil moisture or humidity. Plant it in a well-drained spot, preferably in a raised bed, atop a wall, or near the crest of a slope. In a perennial or herb bed, plant lavender on a small mound to ensure good drainage.

Lavender needs average, light, well-drained soil that is slightly alkaline, with a pH of 6.7 to 7.3; to improve drainage, add builder's sand to the soil before planting. Keep lavender plants mulched as you do other herbs, but never let the mulch touch the crown of the plant. This can encourage rot in winter. A similar problem occurs in the heat of summer, when fungus attacks lavender and turns the leaves brown. As a preventive measure, sprinkle sand around the base of the

AT A GLANCE
❖
LAVENDER
Lavandula species

Features: fragrant herb with purple, pink, or white flowers

Uses: crafts, culinary, landscaping

Type: perennial

Height: 1 to 2½ feet

Width: 1 to 2½ feet

Light: full sun

Soil: average, light, well drained, pH 6.7 to 7.3

Water: low to medium

Range: Zones 5 to 8

Pests: rot

Remarks: drought tolerant, do not overwater

plant to head off moisture from the crown and leaves and to promote fast drainage and quick drying. Do not overwater.

Lavender blooms in late spring and summer, but if you keep faded flowers clipped, plants will bloom intermittently throughout the warm season. Light pruning also encourages branching. Prune stems every spring after new growth begins.

To help lavender and other perennials better survive the winter, sprinkle bonemeal or other fertilizer high in phosphorus around each plant in the fall. Work it into the first inch of soil, or let the rain wash it in.

Grow the least cold-hardy lavenders in containers so that you can overwinter them indoors. Or take cuttings in summer so that by the time you bring them indoors for winter, the cuttings will have developed into well-rooted young plants. Inside, give lavender good air circulation and direct sunlight in a south-facing window. Do not overwater, as this can kill lavender. Allow soil to dry before watering.

Species and Selections

Selections of lavender vary in their flowers, foliage, and fragrance, as well as their adaptability to local climates. As a rule, the selections with the most gray foliage tolerate extremes of heat and cold best and require less water.

Lavender is grown as either a perennial or an annual in the South, depending on the selection and the location. In Zone 8 and farther north, English lavender *(Lavandula angustifolia)* is a handsome perennial, gradually growing larger each year until it reaches 2 feet tall. The foliage is grayish green and aromatic. Try the selections Alba, Hidcote, Jean Davis, Lavender Lady, Munstead, Twickel Purple, and Vera. Hot, humid summers can be hard on English lavender; in Zones 7 and farther south, you may have better luck growing English lavender as an annual.

If you live in the lower South, try newer hybrids such as Provence lavender *(Lavandula x intermedia Provence)*. Other recommended selections include Dutch, Fat Spike, Grosso, and Seal.

Several types of lavender can tolerate the heat and humidity but cannot take the cold. These are good options for gardeners in Zone 8 and farther south, or for gardeners in zones

---

LAVENDER ICE CREAM

1⅓ cups milk
¼ cup honey
4 sprigs fresh lavender
⅔ cup sugar
2 tablespoons all-purpose flour
⅛ teaspoon salt
2 large eggs, beaten
2⅔ cups half-and-half
1 teaspoon vanilla extract
Garnish: fresh lavender flowers

Combine milk and honey in a heavy saucepan, stirring well; add lavender sprigs. Bring to a boil over medium heat, stirring constantly; remove from heat, cover, and cool completely.

Combine sugar, flour, and salt in a bowl; stir well. Remove lavender from milk mixture; gradually stir in sugar mixture. Cook over medium heat, stirring constantly, 8 to 10 minutes or until mixture is thickened and bubbly.

Gradually stir about one-fourth of hot mixture into beaten eggs; add egg mixture to remaining hot mixture, stirring constantly. Cook 2 minutes, stirring constantly. Remove from heat, and cool. Cover and chill thoroughly.

Stir in half-and-half and vanilla. Pour mixture into a 2-quart hand-turned or electric freezer. Freeze according to manufacturer's instructions.

Pack freezer with additional ice and rock salt, and let stand 1 hour before serving. To serve, spoon into individual dessert dishes. Garnish, if desired. Yield: about 1½ quarts.

farther north, who are prepared to grow the plants in containers and bring them indoors for winter. The fringed French lavender *(Lavandula dentata)* features fernlike green or gray foliage and fragrant blooms that open over a long period of time. French lavender tolerates more moisture than other lavenders. Another selection is Spanish lavender *(Lavandula stoechas)*, a gray-leafed plant with needlelike leaves that resemble rosemary leaves.

Harvest, Storage, and Use

You can harvest the aromatic stems of lavender anytime. Use the stems and foliage in potpourris. Cut only every third stem so the plant does not look sheared. Harvest the flowers just before they are fully open, and they will hold their scent for years. Use fresh flowers in desserts, marinades, and sauces.

To dry blossoms for crafts, potpourris, and sachets, gather a bunch of stems and hang them upside down in a dark place, away from sunlight (this will preserve the true color of flowers). Good ventilation will keep bunched stems from molding. Handle dried lavender carefully, as it gets brittle. Put a sachet in the linen closet; lavender is thought to prevent moth damage and mustiness in linens.

This lavender is well placed atop a retaining wall, where drainage and air circulation are good.

Lemon Herbs

Many herbs mimic the flavor of lemon, but among the most true are lemon balm, lemon grass, and lemon verbena. The leaves of these three herbs package the tart taste and scent of lemon in the convenience and attractiveness of a foliage plant. You can enjoy the fruity aromas all summer in the garden and use the leaves for flavoring teas, desserts, and chicken and fish dishes or for making sweetly perfumed sachets.

Lemon Balm

Lemon balm is a thick, bushy plant that grows to 2 feet tall and resembles other members of the mint family with its square stems and opposite paired leaves. Its variegated selections lend contrasting foliage colors to the herb garden.

A member of the mint family, lemon balm is a perennial herb with a mild lemon flavor. Its leaves die back in autumn but return in early spring. Plants are about 2 feet tall and equally wide. Lemon balm can be used as an informal edging plant or in a container.

Planting and Care

Plant lemon balm in the spring as soon as the soil has warmed, placing it in full sun or partial shade. Lemon balm likes rich, well-drained soil with a pH of 6.7 to 7.3. Add a slow-release fertilizer to the soil before or during planting and again each spring.

The easiest way to start lemon balm is from transplants, rooted cuttings, or divisions from an existing plant. If you sow seeds, plant in fall—about four weeks before the first frost. Sow seeds ½ inch deep, and keep the soil evenly moist. Seedlings will germinate in fall, and the small plants will go dormant in winter. In spring, plants will grow quickly. Thin them to 10 to 12 inches apart. Be sure to water lemon balm during dry spells to keep the soil moist, or the plants will wilt.

Pinch back the tips of the stems as the plant grows; this will keep the plant producing more leaves and will prevent flowering. To propagate, divide established plants in spring or fall or make stem cuttings in spring or summer.

Golden lemon balm *(Melissa officinalis Variegata)* is a low-growing form of lemon balm with golden variegated leaves and a light lemon scent. It is perennial in the middle and lower South and requires partial shade (otherwise the leaves will scorch). Some types show the variegation only in early spring or late fall, losing this unique coloring during hot weather. Allgold is also a colorful selection.

For the strongest flavor, use fresh lemon balm.

AT A GLANCE
❖
LEMON BALM
Melissa officinalis

Features: hardy member of the mint family, mild lemon flavor

Uses: crafts, culinary, landscaping

Type: perennial

Height: 2 feet

Width: 2 feet

Light: full sun to partial shade; full shade in Florida and along Gulf Coast

Soil: rich, well drained, pH 6.7 to 7.3

Water: medium to high, do not let soil dry out

Range: Zones 5 to 9

Pests: none specific

Remarks: easy to grow, a must for herb teas, reseeds

LEMON TEA BREAD

¾ cup milk
1 tablespoon chopped fresh
    lemon balm
1 tablespoon chopped fresh
    lemon thyme
½ cup butter or margarine,
    softened
1 cup sugar

2 large eggs
2 cups all-purpose flour
1½ teaspoons baking powder
¼ teaspoon salt
1 tablespoon grated lemon
    rind
Lemon Glaze

Combine first 3 ingredients in a saucepan; bring to a boil. Remove from heat; cover and let stand 5 minutes. Let cool.

Beat butter at medium speed with an electric mixer until creamy; gradually add sugar, beating well. Add eggs, one at a time, beating after each addition.

Combine flour and next 2 ingredients; add to butter mixture alternately with milk mixture, beginning and ending with flour mixture. Mix at low speed after each addition until blended. Stir in lemon rind. Pour batter into a greased and floured 9-x 5-x 3-inch loafpan.

Bake at 325° for 50 minutes or until a wooden pick inserted in center comes out clean. Cool in pan on a wire rack 10 minutes; remove from pan, and cool completely. Spoon Lemon Glaze over bread. Yield: 1 loaf.

Lemon Glaze: Combine 1 cup sifted powdered sugar and 2 tablespoons lemon juice in a small bowl; stir until smooth. Yield: ⅓ cup.

Harvest, Storage, and Use

A native of southern Europe, lemon balm has a mild flavor that blends well with many herbs. Harvest a few leaves at a time, or, in late spring, cut the entire plant back by one-half to two-thirds. The plants will yield at least three more harvests per season. Cutting back leggy plants helps keep them bushy. Remove leaves from the stem, and use them freshly chopped in salads of all types, in steamed vegetables, or as garnishes. Use the leaves to enhance any dish that calls for lemon juice. Fresh sprigs will make a delightful lemon tea. Or freeze leaves in ice cubes and add to cold beverages. Lemon balm can be dried, although it does not hold its fragrance long.

Lemon Grass

Elegant and aromatic, lemon grass is a semi-tropical, grasslike herb whose long leaves are popular in Asian dishes. Lemon grass grows like a giant, billowing grass, reaching 2 to 4 feet tall. It creates a strong, vertical accent in the garden. Use it as an ornamental grass or a specimen plant, or plant it in a container for the deck or patio.

Planting and Care

Lemon grass is easy to grow if started from purchased plants or divisions. Plants grow into a full clump from a single division in one season. This herb requires full sun and average, well-drained soil with a pH of 6.5 to 7.3. Add a slow-release fertilizer before or during planting and again in the spring. Do not overwater.

Perennial in frost-free areas, lemon grass can survive winter in Zone 8 if it is cut back and mulched heavily. If you live in an area that has long, hard freezes, grow lemon grass in a container to overwinter indoors. If the plant is too large to bring indoors, place only a slender division in a container each fall and set it out the following spring after threat of frost has passed.

Harvest, Storage, and Use

Lemon grass has a lemon flavor with a hint of ginger. The flavor and aroma fade quickly, so prepare lemon grass right before you are to use it. (Remove the base and leaves from young plants.) This member of the grass family has sharp reedlike leaves that may cut you if you are not careful. Normally, only about 4 inches of the plant from the bulb up are used. Mash the bulb slightly with the side of a chef's knife, and then thinly slice or sliver the stalk. Use lemon grass in teas, marinades, salad dressings, stir-fry dishes, and curries. It is also good with poultry and seafood. Discard the herb before serving. To use the outer leaves, cut them into ½-inch pieces, dry, and mix into any herb tea blend.

Lemon grass is a tall, grasslike herb. Its striking form makes it a popular ornamental.

LEMON SHRIMP AND PASTA

1½ pounds unpeeled medium-size fresh shrimp
6 stalks lemon grass, thinly sliced (white part only)
1 tablespoon peanut oil
1 cup coconut milk
1½ teaspoons fish sauce
¼ cup thinly sliced green onions
1 tablespoon chopped fresh cilantro
Hot cooked angel hair pasta

Peel and devein shrimp; set aside.

Cook lemon grass in oil in a skillet over medium heat 1 minute, stirring occasionally. Add coconut milk; cook over low heat until reduced by half, stirring occasionally.

Add shrimp; cook 5 minutes or until shrimp turn pink. Stir in fish sauce, green onions, and cilantro; serve immediately over pasta. Yield: 5 to 6 servings.

AT A GLANCE

❖

LEMON GRASS
Cymbopogon citratus

Features: grasslike plant with lemon flavor
Uses: culinary, landscaping
Type: perennial
Height: 2 to 4 feet
Width: 3 feet
Light: full sun
Soil: average, well drained, pH 6.5 to 7.3
Water: medium
Range: Zones 9 and 10
Pests: none specific
Remarks: striking ornamental, popular in Asian cuisine

Lemon verbena produces green foliage with the purest of lemon flavors.

AT A GLANCE
❖

LEMON VERBENA
Aloysia triphylla

Features: tropical shrub with yellow-green foliage, lemon scent and flavor

Uses: crafts, culinary, landscaping

Type: perennial in Zones 8 to 10, annual in Zones 3 to 7

Height: 2 to 5 feet

Width: 1 to 2 feet

Light: full sun

Soil: rich, well drained, pH 6.0 to 7.0

Water: medium

Range: Zones 3 to 10

Pests: none specific

Remarks: good plants for containers

Lemon Verbena

Lemon verbena is a fast-growing tropical that grows to the size of a shrub, from 2 to 5 feet tall depending on the length of the growing season. It is a willowy, informal plant that works well at the back of a border, near steps, or any place where you can grab a fragrant leaf in passing. It is sometimes grown in pots and brought indoors for winter.

Perhaps the most strongly scented of the lemon herbs, lemon verbena has long been prized for use in teas and sachets. Native to Peru, it is a tender perennial in the South, returning each spring in areas where winters are mild (it is hardy to about 25° if heavily mulched). Container plants brought indoors may lose their yellow-green leaves in winter, but the foliage will grow back when the plants are moved outside in spring.

Planting and Care

Plant lemon verbena in the spring after threat of frost has passed. The herb likes full sun and rich, well-drained soil with a pH of 6.0 to 7.0. Add a slow-release fertilizer to the soil before or during planting time, and fertilize with a balanced liquid fertilizer after a heavy harvest. Pinch tips to encourage bushy growth. Lemon verbena can be propagated from cuttings of tender new shoots in July and August.

In the fall, cut back lemon verbena and place in containers to winter indoors. Use the cut leaves for sachets and potpourris. In the spring, cut back weak winter growth on potted plants before setting them out after the last frost.

In Zones 7 and 8, heavily mulch plants left in the ground to protect them through the winter.

Harvest, Storage, and Use

To harvest lemon verbena, snip off stems or pick leaves from woody stems that are too tough to cut. Harvest from spring through early fall; plants will drop their leaves in the fall. Use whole leaves to flavor ice cubes, brew a refreshing tea, or enliven white wine. Add finely chopped leaves to beverages, cakes, ice cream, jams, custards, salad dressings, fruit or vegetable salads, and marinades. Lemon verbena also complements poultry, fish, pork, and veal and can replace lemon in a variety of dishes. It makes a good substitute for lemon grass in Asian recipes. Lemon verbena is an excellent herb for drying for sachets and herb pillows as it holds its fragrance well.

Marjoram

Sweet marjoram resembles oregano but has smaller leaves and a more delicate flavor.

Sweet marjoram, with its gentle, wintergreen scent, is often preferred over oregano as a seasoning. Indeed, sweet marjoram's delicious mellow flavor makes it a versatile herb, one that enhances all types of meats, egg dishes, soups, and vegetables. Since it is a tender perennial, you may have to replant it every spring.

In the Landscape

Sweet marjoram is a low-growing, bushy plant that can reach 1 foot tall. The flower buds, which appear in early summer, look like small knots along the stem, giving the plant its alternate name of "knotted marjoram." The open blooms range in color from white to lilac. Marjoram has sparse, gray-green leaves and does not attract much attention in the landscape. But a group of four or five plants can make a nice edging or ground cover. Marjoram also grows well in containers. Combine it with basil, parsley, and a few summer annuals in a window box.

Planting and Care

Plant sweet marjoram in full sun to partial shade. Since sweet marjoram is slow growing, it is best to start with transplants. Plant these in the spring after threat of frost has passed.

Sweet marjoram is perennial in Zones 8 and 9, although it may need the protection of mulch in winter. In Zone 7, mulch is essential to insulate the tender roots from cold, and even then it will not always survive winter. In Zone 6 and farther north, sweet marjoram becomes a summer annual. In South Florida, it is a winter annual, as it will succumb to heat and humidity in summer.

Sweet marjoram likes rich, well-drained soil with a pH of 6.7 to 7.0. Add a slow-release fertilizer to the soil before or during planting. Trim plants before they flower and fertilize again with a balanced liquid fertilizer. Water during periods of extended drought, but be careful not to overwater; a native of the Mediterranean, sweet marjoram prefers a slightly dry climate.

If you live north of Zone 7, dig plants out of the ground in late fall, or plant cuttings from late spring to midsummer and overwinter them indoors. You may also divide marjoram in spring or fall to start new plants.

AT A GLANCE

❖

MARJORAM, SWEET
Origanum majorana

Features: low-growing, bushy herb with mellow flavor

Uses: culinary

Type: annual in Zones 3 to 7 and 10, perennial in Zones 8 and 9

Height: 1 foot

Width: 6 to 10 inches

Light: full sun to partial shade

Soil: rich, light, well drained, pH 6.7 to 7.0

Water: low to medium

Range: Zones 3 to 10

Pests: none specific

Remarks: cannot tolerate extreme cold or heat

GRILLED TENDERLOIN WITH SAUTÉED MUSHROOMS

4 cloves garlic, crushed
½ teaspoon salt, divided
¾ teaspoon freshly ground pepper, divided
6 beef tenderloin steaks (about 2 pounds)
1 tablespoon vegetable oil
1½ pounds medium-size fresh mushrooms, sliced
¼ cup butter or margarine, melted
2½ teaspoons minced fresh sweet marjoram
¼ cup dry sherry
Vegetable cooking spray

Rub garlic, ¼ teaspoon salt, and ½ teaspoon pepper evenly over both sides of steaks; brush both sides with oil. Cover and let stand 10 minutes.

Cook mushrooms in butter in a large skillet over medium-high heat, stirring constantly, 1 minute. Stir in remaining ¼ teaspoon salt and ¼ teaspoon pepper, marjoram, and sherry; bring to a boil. Reduce heat, and simmer, uncovered, stirring occasionally, until mushrooms are tender and liquid is slightly reduced (about 5 to 7 minutes). Remove from heat; cover and keep warm.

Coat grill rack with cooking spray; place on grill over medium-hot coals (350° to 400°). Place steaks on rack, and cook 4 minutes on each side or to desired degree of doneness. Serve mushrooms over steaks. Yield: 6 servings.

Species and Selections

Sweet marjoram *(Origanum majorana)* is the most widely grown marjoram. Another popular type is evergreen marjoram *(Origanum majoricum)*. Its flavor and aroma are comparable to sweet marjoram. This species prefers sun or partial shade and well-drained soil. It is an evergreen perennial in Zone 6 and south, and in Zone 5 it may come back from the roots each spring. You can propagate it by rooting cuttings or making divisions in early spring. (See page 32 for more about propagation.)

Harvest, Storage, and Use

Four to six weeks after you plant marjoram, begin harvesting it by picking fresh leaves as needed. Do not remove more than one-third of the leaves from a plant at one harvest. Make a second harvest when flowers reappear later in the season.

Dried marjoram retains its full flavor. If you plan to dry marjoram, harvest after flower buds form but before they open. Strip leaves from the stems after drying.

Add marjoram sparingly near the end of the cooking process. Its mild spicy flavor is particularly good with vegetables such as beans, peas, carrots, and spinach. Add it to salads and butters for use on fish, and in tomato, egg, and cheese dishes. Use it in oil and vinegar salad dressings.

Sweet marjoram is a low-growing, bushy plant suited for edging the garden.

Mint

Once you have grown accustomed to drinking iced mint tea on a hot summer day, you will never want to be without fresh mint. A hardy perennial, it is one of the easiest and most versatile herbs to grow. From a culinary standpoint, mint is a wonderful addition to everything from lamb to white wine vinegar. You may have a difficult time choosing which of the many types to grow—aromas and flavors range from apple to spearmint to chocolate.

In the Landscape

Mint is a spreading perennial that loves damp areas in the garden. Most types die back in winter, except pineapple mint, which is evergreen in the mild winters of the lower South. Mint grows 12 to 15 inches tall and spreads rapidly by stems that creep above and just below the soil surface. It will form large patches and may become invasive, so choose a site where it can grow with abandon. To control spreading, plant mint in a confined space, such as a strip of ground between a paved walk and the house foundation, or in containers or in pots sunk in the ground. Curly mint, orange mint, peppermint, and spearmint spread the most rapidly.

Mint blooms from June through September in whorls of small flowers. You may want to pinch off the flowers before they open to help the plant stay as neat and compact as possible.

Planting and Care

Plant mint where it will get plenty of moisture. It will grow in full sun or shade. Fertile, well-drained soil with a pH of 6.0 to 7.0 is ideal although mint will grow well even in poor soil. Water mint at least one inch per week; do not allow soil to dry out. Mulch to help keep roots moist.

The easiest way to start mint is from transplants or from runners taken from an existing plant. These runners creep along the ground to form a mat, rooting as they go. You can sever a rooted runner from its parent plant and set it out as you would a transplant, being careful to bury the small roots completely. Leave at least 1 foot between plants of the same type and 4 feet between different types. If plants become crowded, use a shovel or a spade to cut the runners between plants, removing the ones that have wandered out-of-bounds.

Eventually, the flavor and fragrance of a patch of mint will diminish and the patch may begin to die out. Lift the plants out of the soil and reset every three or four years.

Give all mints, including peppermint, a spot of their own where they can spread without overtaking other plants.

AT A GLANCE
❖
MINT
Mentha species

Features: bushy foliage plant with refreshing flavors

Uses: crafts, culinary, landscaping

Type: perennial

Height: 12 to 15 inches

Width: spreads indefinitely

Light: full sun to shade

Soil: fertile, moist, well drained, pH 6.0 to 7.0

Water: medium to high

Range: Zones 5 to 9

Pests: none specific

Remarks: spreads easily, tolerates soggy soil

MINTED MELON SALAD

1¼ cups sugar
½ cup water
⅔ cup loosely packed fresh mint leaves
2 cups cantaloupe balls
1 cup honeydew melon balls
1 cup watermelon balls
Curly leaf lettuce leaves

Combine sugar and water in a small saucepan. Bring to a boil over medium heat; boil, uncovered, 1 minute or until sugar dissolves, stirring occasionally. Remove from heat.

Combine sugar mixture and mint leaves in container of an electric blender; cover and process until mint leaves are finely chopped.

Combine cantaloupe, honeydew, and watermelon balls with mint syrup mixture in a large bowl; toss gently. Cover and chill at least 2 hours. Serve over lettuce leaves. Yield: 4 servings.

For a colorful combination, pair pineapple mint with yellow coreopsis.

Species and Selections

Some of the most popular types include mints with distinctive flavors. Peppermint *(Mentha* x *piperita)* is the source of true peppermint flavor. It has narrow, dark green leaves with purple stems and grows about 2 feet tall.

Spearmint *(Mentha spicata),* with its sharp, clean aroma, is the mint used in spearmint flavorings. Growing 2 to 2½ feet tall, it is characterized by reddish stems, finely toothed, pointed leaves, and lavender flowers. Spearmint spreads rapidly and may be evergreen where winters are mild.

Orange mint, or bergamot *(Mentha* x *piperita Citrata)*, has a strong citrus aroma. It grows 1 to 2 feet tall and has reddish green stems, purple-edged leaves, and purple flowers. It spreads rapidly but is not as invasive as other mints.

Apple mint *(Mentha suaveolens)* has rounded woolly leaves with a slight apple scent. It grows 2 to 3 feet tall with upright, stiff stems and gray-white blossoms touched with pink. It does better than other mints under dry conditions and spreads only moderately.

Pineapple mint *(Mentha suaveolens* Variegata), a cousin of the woolly apple mint, has cream-and-green-splotched leaves with a pleasant, fruity aroma. The most ornamental of all mints, it will reach 18 inches in height and needs partial shade to retain its coloration. It is evergreen during mild winters but should be mulched for protection. Pineapple mint spreads slowly.

Chocolate mint *(Mentha* x *piperita* Chocolate) tastes and smells like an after-dinner mint. Serve it on ice cream or as a garnish on cakes.

Harvest, Storage, and Use

Harvest mint anytime from early spring into late fall. The flavor in the leaves is most concentrated just before flowering, so you may want to harvest then, cutting the entire plant to just above the first or second pair of leaves. Since the lower leaves begin to turn yellow around this time too, the harvest will help to neaten the garden and produce bushier plants. You can usually make three such harvests per season.

Use mint fresh, frozen, or dried. Add fresh mint to vegetables, lamb, fish, poultry, salads, sauces, and teas, punches, or other beverages. Freeze in ice cube trays, or preserve in vinegar. Include dried mint for use in potpourris and herb sachets.

Oregano

Native from Europe to Central Asia, the numerous types of oregano give you interesting options in the garden as well as in the kitchen. Some, such as golden oregano, are grown for their ornamental qualities. Others, such as Cuban oregano and Mexican oregano, are not true oreganos but are used like them. Italian and Greek oreganos are the preferred culinary types, their pungent flavor being an essential ingredient in Italian, Asian, Spanish, and Mexican cuisines.

In the Landscape

Most oreganos are shrubby plants that grow from 6 inches to 2 feet and have small, round, green leaves. While not particularly flashy, the larger plants provide a nice foil to brightly colored flowers, such as marigold or golden yarrow. Some oreganos have trailing habits that make them suitable as a ground cover or as an edging along a walkway. In the lower South, they may be evergreen. All selections spread easily and are drought tolerant, making them excellent for containers. Plants flower from July to September and feature small rose to white blossoms.

Planting and Care

Oregano likes full sun but will also grow in afternoon shade in Zone 7 and farther south. The best way to start oregano is from transplants. Plant in well-drained soil with a pH of 6.0 to 7.0. Add a slow-release

Oregano's small leaves give the plant a fine texture.

In the landscape, use oregano as a green foil for flowering herbs and perennials. Grow it in full sun or partial shade.

AT A GLANCE

OREGANO
Origanum species

Features: bushy, green-leafed plant with aromatic foliage and robust flavor

Uses: crafts, culinary

Type: tender perennial

Height: ½ to 2 feet

Width: 1 to 2 feet

Light: full sun to partial shade

Soil: average, well drained, pH 6.0 to 7.0

Water: medium

Range: Zones 5 to 9

Pests: aphids, fungus, root rot, spider mites

Remarks: easy to grow, essential culinary herb

fertilizer before or during planting and work in again each spring.

Most types of oregano send out runners that will root as they grow; separate and transplant these. To start new plants, root stem cuttings taken in the spring or fall. Oregano can be grown from seed, but do not collect seeds from plants in the garden; purchase them. Plants in the garden often cross-pollinate, yielding unexpected results.

Harvest oregano often to encourage tender new growth. In the fall, remove tender selections from the ground to overwinter indoors. Plants left outside should be protected by mulch or a cold frame. Remove dead stems in the spring before new growth appears.

Greek oregano is the most popular oregano for cooking because of its strong flavor and aromatic leaves.

Species and Selections

There are several types of oregano whose appearance is easily confused with sweet marjoram. (See the Marjoram profile on page 91.) Some of the plants listed here are used as substitutes for oregano, but they belong to a different botanical genus.

Although oregano *(Origanum species)* is classified as a perennial, the least cold-hardy types are grown as annuals. Some oreganos are evergreen in the South, while others can be killed by frost.

Native to Greece, Greek oregano *(Origanum vulgare Hirtum)* is listed also as *Origanum heracleoticum* and is a popular selection of culinary oregano. Greek oregano is grown for its strong flavor and aromatic leaves. It is a tender perennial and needs to be protected with mulch in the winter in Zone 7 and south. Farther north, treat it as an annual. Greek oregano grows about 12 inches tall, with small, bright green leaves and white flowers. If grown with other selections, it will be overrun by the more vigorous, larger-leafed types. To promote a bushier plant, cut it back to one-third its size in late spring.

Italian oregano *(Origanum x majoricum)* is one of the most popular oreganos for culinary use. A perennial that grows 12 to 18 inches tall, Italian oregano has a flavor that is stronger than sweet marjoram but milder than Greek oregano. It is not reliably hardy north of Zone 6.

Also called Spanish oregano, wild marjoram *(Origanum vulgare)* is a hardy perennial that is evergreen through mild winters in the South. It is the most common oregano grown but not always the cook's favorite as its flavor can vary from weak to strong, depending upon the selection. Plants are bushy and shrublike, growing 1 to 3 feet tall, and bearing lavender or pink flowers in clusters, which are commonly dried and used as everlastings. This marjoram is often sold as seeds in packets and through mail order catalogues.

Golden oregano *(Origanum vulgare Aureum)* is a form of wild marjoram. It is grown as an ornamental and works well as a ground cover in shady areas. This oregano is not good for culinary use.

Although it is called marjoram, pot marjoram *(Origanum onites)* is a species of oregano. It has a sharp flavor that is stronger than other types when its leaves are used fresh. Pot marjoram is a shrubby perennial, growing to 2 feet tall with small gray-green leaves. If left outside in Zone 6 and north, pot marjoram will not survive the freezing temperatures.

Cuban oregano *(Plecthranthus ambonicus)*, also listed as *Coleus amboinicus* or Spanish thyme, is not a true oregano, but it is a good substitute for Mediterranean oreganos. Fragrant, large-leafed, and frequently variegated, Cuban oregano is a tender perennial that cannot tolerate frost; grow it as an annual or in containers. Its large, succulent leaves are tolerant of sun and drought.

Mexican oregano *(Poliomintha longiflora)* is a strong-smelling plant popular in Mexico and Texas. Excellent for hot, humid areas, this woody shrub grows 3 feet tall. The small green leaves yield an essential oil similar to that of oregano and are used in cooking. Its tubular flowers of white to lavender blue attract hummingbirds.

Harvest, Storage, and Use

Harvest sprigs of oregano as soon as the plants reach 6 inches in height. If you want to harvest a large amount for drying, wait until just before plants bloom in midsummer. The flavor is most concentrated at this time. Cut the stems above the lowest set of leaves. Make another cutting in late summer after new foliage has sprouted.

Add oregano to Italian dishes, meat, cheese, fish, eggs, fresh and cooked tomatoes, zucchini, black beans, snap beans, and marinades. Sprinkle it lightly over salads before adding the dressing.

Use the flower stalks of oregano in wreaths and other crafts. Dry the foliage of Italian or Greek oregano for future culinary use. Strip leaves from stems after drying and store them refrigerated or frozen. (See page 39 for information on drying herbs.)

Troubleshooting

Oregano can suffer from aphids, fungus, root rot, and spider mites. To prevent disease, provide excellent drainage and remove diseased foliage promptly. See pages 124-125 for more information.

WHITE LIGHTNING TEXAS CHILI

1 pound dried navy beans
4 (14½-ounce) cans ready-to-serve chicken broth, divided
1 large onion, chopped
2 cloves garlic, minced
1 tablespoon ground white pepper
2½ tablespoons fresh oregano
1 tablespoon ground cumin
½ teaspoon ground cloves
5 cups chopped cooked chicken
2 (4½-ounce) cans chopped green chiles, undrained
1 cup water
1 teaspoon salt
1 jalapeño pepper, seeded and chopped
Shredded Monterey Jack cheese
Salsa
Sour cream
Sliced green onions

Sort and wash beans; place in a large Dutch oven. Cover with water 2 inches above beans; let soak 8 hours. Drain beans, and return to Dutch oven. Add 3 cans chicken broth, chopped onion, and next 5 ingredients. Bring to a boil; cover, reduce heat, and simmer 2 hours or until beans are tender.

Add remaining can of chicken broth, chicken, and next 4 ingredients. Bring to a boil; cover, reduce heat, and simmer 1 hour, stirring occasionally. Serve with cheese, salsa, sour cream, and green onions. Yield: 11 cups.

Parsley

Curly parsley is a striking ornamental both in the garden and as a garnish.

The emerald green foliage of parsley looks as good edging a garden as it does garnishing a plate. A native of Europe, parsley traditionally has been grown as a culinary herb, but its ability to tolerate mild freezes as well as summer heat makes it a popular addition to flower beds. Its attractiveness to the parsleyworm, a pretty caterpillar that eventually turns into a black swallowtail butterfly, is another reason to select it for your herb garden.

Parsley comes in many selections, including a savory curly-leafed type. Mild, peppery parsley foliage is an ingredient in a variety of dishes. The fresh leaves and strongly flavored stems can also be eaten as a natural breath freshener.

In the Landscape

Depending on the selection, parsley has curly or flat leaves and grows 1 to 2 feet tall. It is evergreen in much of the South. Plant parsley as an edging plant or as a companion to colorful annuals, such as yellow pansies or pink petunias, which bring out its rich green luster. Parsley is also an ideal plant to combine with flowers in containers.

Planting and Care

Parsley is a biennial, growing only leaves the first year and then blooming, setting seed, and dying the second year. Although biennial, it is usually grown as an annual planted in spring or sometimes in fall. It flourishes in cool weather. In Zone 7 and south, parsley is a good addition to the fall garden because it stays green through the winter. Farther north, parsley is planted in spring because it dies back in the winter unless it is protected by a cold frame.

Plant parsley in full sun or partial shade. The easiest and quickest way to start parsley is from very young transplants. However, you can grow it from seed, which is often sold in nurseries and supermarkets. If you sow seeds, it is best to start them directly in the ground in late winter or early spring, because plants develop a long taproot that makes transplanting difficult. Parsley seeds are slow to sprout; soak them in warm water for 24 hours before planting to help speed germination. Do not cover seeds with soil, as the seeds need light to sprout. Keep the soil moist; seeds will not germinate if left to dry out. Thin and transplant seedlings when they are 1 inch tall.

Parsley likes a rich, moist soil with a pH of 5.5 to 6.7. Add a slow-release fertilizer to the soil before or during planting.

Water once a week, but never allow parsley leaves to wilt or turn yellow. Mulch will keep parsley roots cool and moist, but do not let it touch the crown of the plant as rot may develop.

Parsley planted in fall will flower in early summer. You can remove the flower stems to encourage new foliage and lengthen the plant's life into summer although the leaves will be tough. The yellow flowers will set seed and self-sow if not kept trimmed.

In September, cut back spring-planted parsley to encourage new growth. Parsley planted the previous fall is best replaced with new transplants.

Species and Selections

Curly parsley *(Petroselinum crispum var. crispum)* is commonly used as a garnish and in salads. Its bright green, tightly curled leaves are also popular in flower beds, especially as a green foil for pansies in winter. Curly parsley grows 10 to 12 inches tall. Selections include Extra Curled Dwarf and Evergreen (which is green through mild winters, even in the upper South).

Known for its stronger and superior flavor that is not lost during cooking, Italian parsley *(Petroselinum crispum var. neopolitanum)* is used primarily for seasoning, especially in Italian and Middle Eastern dishes. Italian parsley has flat leaves and will grow to 2 feet tall. It is easier to grow than curly parsley in Zone 7 and farther south as it withstands the heat of long southern summers.

A fragile herb, chervil *(Anthriscus cerefolium)* is commonly known as French parsley and is grown as an annual in the South (it

Italian parsley's foliage does not lose much of its flavor when heated.

TABBOULEH

½ cup bulgur (cracked wheat), uncooked

1 cup water

3 cups finely shredded lettuce

2 cups tightly packed, chopped fresh parsley (about 1½ large bunches)

2 large tomatoes, seeded and finely chopped

1 small onion, minced

¼ cup chopped fresh mint

1 clove garlic, minced

¼ cup lemon juice

2 tablespoons olive oil

1 teaspoon salt

½ teaspoon pepper

Combine bulgur and water in a medium bowl; cover and let stand 1 hour or until water is absorbed. Drain bulgur well, and squeeze dry in paper towels.

Press lettuce and parsley between paper towels to remove excess moisture; place in a large bowl. Add bulgur, tomato, and next 3 ingredients; toss gently.

Combine lemon juice and remaining 3 ingredients in a small bowl. Stir well with a wire whisk. Pour dressing over bulgur mixture; toss gently. Cover and chill 1 hour. Toss again just before serving. Yield: 6 cups.

is biennial in the North). Chervil reaches about 1½ feet tall in partial shade. Start it from seed in the early fall in Zone 8 and farther south, or in the spring farther north. Plant in moist, rich soil with a pH of 6.5. Fertilize with a slow-release fertilizer before planting. Chervil can withstand temperatures as low as 25 degrees and may be harvested throughout the winter in many areas of the South. It flowers in spring and will set seed and die by summer, frequently self-sowing.

Harvest, Storage, and Use

Harvest the fresh leaves and stems of parsley as you need them. Snip the leaf stalks from the outside, cutting at the base, not more than 1 inch above the soil. This low clipping encourages bushier plants. If you keep the flower stalks cut, the plants may last several years, although they will grow weaker over time. If you live where parsley is not evergreen, freeze it for winter use. You can easily dry parsley, but it will not retain much flavor. Eat the flower stalks as you would celery.

Rich in vitamins A, B, and C, parsley contributes nutrients as well as color to foods. Always add parsley near the end of the cooking process, or sprinkle finely chopped parsley on vegetables or salads just before serving. Use parsley in bouquets garnis, egg dishes, soups, vegetables, rice, potato and pasta dishes, meat, herbal butters, and cottage cheese.

Harvest and use fresh chervil as you would parsley. Chervil has a subtle anise flavor and is best fresh or cooked only briefly. Add chervil to egg dishes, soups, fish sauces, and salads.

Troubleshooting

Parsley attracts the parsleyworm that will chew on the plants. Although they can strip leaves, you certainly do not want to kill these caterpillars for they will turn into black swallowtail butterflies. The best control is to add a few extra parsley plants for the caterpillars. Parsley may also be bothered by whiteflies. Chervil may be bothered by aphids. See pages 124-125 for more information on pests.

To harvest parsley, clip stalks at the base of the plant.

Rosemary

Rosemary has many culinary and ornamental uses. In the lower South, it is a handsome evergreen shrub. Rub its leaves and a pine fragrance fills the air. Rosemary's unique aroma and flavor accent a variety of foods and crafts.

In the Landscape

A slow-growing, upright, bushy herb, rosemary often reaches 3 to 5 feet tall after several years of growth. The stems become woody with age and are covered with green needlelike foliage. Prostrate or creeping selections range from tiny small-leafed plants suitable for bonsai to large-leafed plants usable as a ground cover on a dry hillside. These rarely grow taller than 1 to 2 feet, with short, narrow leaves. They make excellent container plants, topiaries, or edgings for rock walls and terraces in the warmer areas of the lower South.

Rosemary flowers vary from white to pink to blue, and the blooming time depends on the selection. Plants that bloom in late spring or early summer attract bees; those that bloom in November and December are a delight during the winter holidays. Use rosemary as an evergreen hedge in Zone 8 and south. Farther north, grow rosemary in a container and bring it indoors to overwinter.

Planting and Care

This evergreen perennial thrives without winter protection in Zone 8 and farther south. In Zones 6 and 7, it may be damaged by severe freezes. Heavy mulching helps rosemary survive through winter, as does planting it beside a south-facing masonry wall. The wall will absorb the sun's warmth and radiate heat at night, as well as shield the plant from north winds. If you live in a windy location, always choose a protected spot for your rosemary, because extreme cold in Zones 8 and 9 can kill the tops of this herb. Keep a rosemary plant in a container year-round in case plants in the ground are lost during a hard winter. However, beware that if the soil in the pot dries out and the plant wilts, rosemary does not recover.

Rosemary likes full sun but will tolerate partial shade. The best way to start rosemary is from transplants. Set plants out in spring as soon as the soil warms or in early fall. Rosemary needs light soil with a pH of 6.0 to 6.7; add lime, if necessary. Rosemary is suited to raised beds or containers as it requires good drainage. Mix a slow-release fertilizer with the soil before or during planting, and fertilize again the following spring.

Unlike most herbs, rosemary has a stronger flavor when fresh than when dried. Cut fresh sprigs anytime.

AT A GLANCE

❖

ROSEMARY
Rosmarinus officinalis

Features: shrubby evergreen herb, pine scent

Uses: crafts, culinary, landscaping

Type: perennial

Height: 1 to 5 feet

Width: 2 to 4 feet

Light: full sun to partial shade

Soil: light, well drained, pH 6.0 to 6.7

Water: medium

Range: Zones 4 to 9, evergreen perennial in Zones 8 to 10

Pests: powdery mildew, root rot, mealybugs, spider mites, whiteflies

Remarks: traditional favorite, ideal for containers

The key to growing healthy rosemary is well-drained soil that stays evenly moist, as in this raised brick planting bed.

Layering is an almost foolproof method of obtaining new plants once you have a planting started. (See page 33 for more about layering.) You can also start new plants from stem cuttings in spring and summer. Starting from seed is not practical; seeds are slow to germinate, and the rate of germination is poor. It takes three years to produce a good-sized plant from seed, and seeds do not produce a predictable, dependable clone.

Rosemary likes evenly moist soil but is susceptible to root rot if kept too wet. Let the soil surface dry out between waterings. Mulch to keep roots moist in summer and protected in winter, but do not allow the mulch to touch the crown of the plant. Prune dead wood in the spring.

If you live in an area north of Zone 8, move rosemary to a protected location or bring it indoors for winter. Place in a cool spot, about 45 degrees, with bright sunlight. Water infrequently—just enough to keep the soil moist.

Species and Selections

Many selections of rosemary are available. These vary in form, flavor, flower color, and winter hardiness. Check with local sources for recommendations of selections that perform well in your area. Arp and Old Salem are upright selections considered to be among the hardiest. Prostrate types are generally less cold hardy and should be grown in

Rosemary grows well in containers, making it possible for gardeners in cold climates to bring the herb indoors in the winter.

containers or hanging baskets that can be moved to a protected location. While most types have pale lavender flowers, some selections of rosemary, such as Benenden Blue, Santa Barbara, Collingwood Ingram, and Tuscan Blue, have blue blooms that are quite showy. Try Albus for white blooms or Majorca Pink or Corsicus for pink.

Harvest, Storage, and Use

For fresh use, cut stems anytime. To dry the leaves, harvest just before the plant blooms. The flavor will be stronger, and it is the best time to prune plants. Dry stems on a rack, or bunch several sprigs and hang them to dry. Then strip the leaves from the stem. Rosemary sprigs also can be frozen or stored in vinegars and refrigerated oils.

Rosemary's strong flavor combines well with other herbs, but use its leaves sparingly. Strip fresh leaves from stems, chop, and add as an accent in soups, meats, stews, or vegetables. Work rosemary into bread dough, or mix it with wine or olive oil and garlic for a marinade.

Rosemary can become a simple luxury when you drop a sprig into bathwater, add it to a bouquet, or wrap it around a napkin ring. Fresh rosemary works well in wreaths. Use dried rosemary in sachets. Burn a bunch of rosemary branches over charcoal when grilling to enhance the flavor of foods.

Troubleshooting

Rosemary is susceptible to powdery mildew and root rot, especially along the Gulf Coast. As a preventive measure, provide excellent drainage and good air circulation. Always clean the garden thoroughly in the fall, and promptly remove any diseased plants. Mealybugs, spider mites, and whiteflies can also be a problem. See pages 124-125 for more information about these pests and diseases.

MARINATED BROILED LAMB CHOPS

1 tablespoon chopped fresh
   rosemary
½ teaspoon freshly ground
   pepper
¼ teaspoon salt
2 cloves garlic, crushed
4 (5-ounce) lamb chops
Vegetable cooking spray
Garnish: fresh rosemary sprigs

Mash rosemary, pepper, salt, and garlic to a paste. Rub garlic mixture over both sides of chops; cover and chill 30 minutes. Place chops on rack of a broiler pan coated with cooking spray. Broil 5½ inches from heat (with electric oven door partially opened) 5 to 6 minutes on each side or to desired degree of doneness. Garnish, if desired. Yield: 4 servings.

To harvest rosemary, gently strip fresh leaves from the stem.

Sage

Golden sage not only brightens the garden, but also is an excellent container plant.

Sage offers you handsome evergreen foliage in the form of a small mounding shrub. Sage is perennial in most areas of the South and comes in colorful selections, including golden, green, white, variegated, tricolor, and purple sage. Not to be confused with flowering salvias, which are ornamental and also called sages, garden sage is used to flavor foods and is essential to many poultry and holiday recipes.

In the Landscape

Native to the Mediterranean, garden sage forms a sprawling shrub 8 to 36 inches tall and wide. Its velvety gray-green color blends well with the deeper greens of perennials or other herbs. Golden sage brightens the garden with yellow green leaves that are as striking as flowers; it is popular mixed into a flower or herb border. The darker shade of purple sage blends well with other Mediterranean herbs, such as purple basil, rosemary, or silver-leafed plants like artemisia.

Planting and Care

In Zone 7 and north, sage is a hardy perennial, its leaves lingering on the stems through the winter. But sage usually does not survive the hot, humid summers of Zone 8 and farther south and is grown as a cool-weather annual in these areas.

Sage needs full sun to partial shade. For quickest results, start with purchased transplants in spring or fall. Plant sage in well-drained, sandy soil with a pH of 6.0 to 6.7. Add a slow-release fertilizer to the soil at planting, and fertilize each spring. Add sand along with organic matter to clay soil to improve drainage.

To grow transplants from seed, start indoors six to eight weeks before the last frost, and set out transplants when the ground is warm. Or sow seeds directly in the garden after danger of frost is past, planting them about ¼ inch deep. Seedlings should appear in two to three weeks. When they are about 2 inches tall, thin to 18 to 24 inches. You can also root your stem cuttings in late spring to start your own transplants. Yet another way to propagate sage is to layer side branches. (See page 32 for more about propagation.)

The foliage of sage looks lifeless through winter and into spring, so prune plants each year in early spring cutting out the oldest growth to help stimulate new growth. In late spring, spikes of pinkish purple flowers will appear.

Sage also grows well in containers. Dig small plants from the garden or sow seeds directly in a container and place in full sun.

Species and Selections

Tricolor sage *(Salvia officinalis* Tricolor) grows to 15 inches and has gray leaves streaked with purple and white. It has the same flavor as garden sage but is less cold hardy.

Growing to 15 inches tall with purple leaves, purple sage *(Salvia officinalis* Purpurea) has the same flavor as garden sage but is slightly hardier.

Often used in confined areas and as a winter houseplant, dwarf sage *(Salvia officinalis* Compacta) grows 8 inches tall. It is a miniature of garden sage, with the same gray-green color and traditional flavor. Dwarf sage performs better in Southern gardens and is more attractive year-round than garden sage. Berggarten is a selection that performs especially well in the South.

Golden sage *(Salvia officinalis* Aurea) grows to 15 inches with yellow-edged leaves. It is popular as an ornamental.

Purple sage, shown here with parsley, is a culinary herb that doubles as an ornamental.

Harvest, Storage, and Use

Lightly harvest plants the first year and then harvest as needed year-round; frequent harvesting helps keep the plant shapely. Pinch one leaf at a time, or cut an entire stem for a larger harvest. Allow two months between the last harvest and the first frost to ensure that new growth will have time to mature in winter.

Use sage fresh, dried, or frozen. To dry sage, hang stems in bunches; when leaves are dry, strip them from the stem and store. If you plan to use sage in dried herb arrangements, let the flowers remain on the plant to develop an attractive pod before you harvest.

Troubleshooting

Sage is susceptible to rot and mildew. Keep plants thinned to provide good air circulation. Even then, sage may succumb to humidity in midsummer.

PEAR AND HAZELNUT DRESSING

1 pound ground pork sausage	2 large sweet red peppers, chopped
4 stalks celery, sliced	
1 large onion, chopped	1 cup toasted, chopped hazelnuts
½ cup butter or margarine, melted	3 tablespoons chopped fresh sage
2 large red pears, chopped	2 teaspoons coarsely ground pepper
4 cloves garlic, minced	1½ cups turkey or chicken broth
1 (16-ounce) loaf day-old French bread, cubed	

Brown pork sausage in a large skillet, stirring until it crumbles. Drain sausage on paper towels. Discard drippings.

Cook celery and onion in butter in large skillet over medium-high heat, stirring constantly, until tender. Add chopped pear and garlic; cook, stirring constantly, until pear is tender. Remove pear mixture from heat.

Place French bread cubes in a large bowl. Stir in sausage, pear mixture, sweet pepper, and next 3 ingredients. Add broth, stirring gently. Spoon into a lightly greased 13- x 9- x 2-inch baking dish. Bake, uncovered, at 350° for 40 minutes. Serve with roast turkey. Yield: 12 servings.

Salvia

AT A GLANCE
❖
SALVIA
Salvia species

Features: natural, shrublike plant with dramatic fall and summer flowers

Uses: culinary (pineapple sage), landscaping

Type: annual and perennial

Height: 2 to 10 feet

Width: 2 to 4 feet

Light: full sun to partial shade

Soil: moderately rich, well drained, pH 6.4

Water: medium

Range: Zones 5 to 10

Pests: whiteflies

Remarks: easy to grow, good value for little effort

A host of flowering salvias reach a second peak from late summer to early fall, bringing color, hummingbirds, and butterflies to the garden. From aromatic and edible pineapple sage to handsome and exotic Mexican bush sage, ornamental salvias stand tall with spikes of blue, purple, pink, white, or red. A few are perennial only in Zone 8 and farther south. Remember that these ornamentals, while called sage, differ from garden sage which is edible. (See pages 104-105.) However, you will want salvias in your garden as they are fast-growing and provide brilliant color for little effort.

In the Landscape

Salvias grow in a single season from 2 to 10 feet tall, depending on the selection, making impressive specimens in your garden. These shrublike plants serve well in a grouping at the back of a mixed herb and flower border or in colorful rows along a fence. For contrast, pair blue and purple salvias with strong yellow flowers, such as marigolds, rudbeckia, sunflowers, or yarrow.

Planting and Care

Most salvias need full sun for at least six hours a day for best flowering; they will tolerate partial afternoon shade. You can easily grow them from transplants in the spring after threat of frost has passed.

Salvias like moderately rich, well-drained soil with a pH of about 6.4. Good drainage is a must. If you have heavy clay soil, add sand, fine gravel, or organic matter to improve drainage. Fertilize with a slow-release fertilizer before planting and again each spring for perennials.

You must provide plenty of water during summer, especially in August. Many salvias are drought tolerant, but they still need ample water for rapid growth. Taller plants may require staking, although pinching back the outer branches can help support the inner stalks. Plants may need occasional pruning to keep them looking neat.

Cut back perennial types after frost, and mulch for protection from winter cold.

You can propagate salvias by cuttings or division. Divide clumps in spring or fall. For salvias that are tender perennials, take 4- to 6-inch cuttings (remove the flower stalks) and set them in containers filled with one part moist sand or perlite and one part commercial soilless growing medium. Most transplants will root within a month in warm weather and can be brought indoors in fall. Overwinter them indoors by a basement window or in a greenhouse.

Species and Selections

The popular annual salvia *(Salvia splendens)* is commonly used as a bedding plant for summer color, as is culinary sage *(Salvia officinalis)*. Do not confuse these two with other salvias, most of which are perennial in mild climates and perform differently.

Texas sage *(Salvia coccinea)*, also called scarlet sage, is typically grown as an annual and is one of the best hummingbird and butterfly plants for the herb garden. Native to the Southwest, it reaches 2 feet tall and features tubular red flowers full of nectar. Lady in Red is an award-winning red selection that produces neat, compact plants suitable for containers. Coral Nymph is a bicolored selection in salmon and white. Texas sage easily reseeds, blooms from early summer to frost, and looks great massed in a bed or at the back of a perennial border.

A fall-blooming salvia, Mexican bush or velvet sage *(Salvia leucantha)*, sports thin gray-green leaves and spikes of soft, fuzzy purple flowers atop 15- to 20- inch spikes. Plants grow 3 to 5 feet tall. Winter hardy to Zone 7, this herb attracts bees and hummingbirds. Emerald is a selection with purple flowers and white centers.

With some of the showiest flowers of all the salvias and leaves that have a faint, spicy scent, anise sage *(Salvia guaranitica)* is a magnet for hummingbirds. Wisps of 1½- to 2-inch-long bluish purple flowers appear on 3-foot-high plants throughout the summer. One selection, Late Blooming Giant, reaches 9 or 10 feet. Anise sage is a tender perennial north of Zone 7, dying back at frost and reappearing again in early spring.

Texas sage offers flowers in the truest of reds.

With some of the largest blooms of any salvia, anise sage draws hummingbirds to the herb garden.

Native to the South, autumn sage *(Salvia greggii)*, or cherry sage as it is sometimes called, is found primarily in Texas. This 2- to 3-foot shrub thrives across the lower and middle South, where it blooms profusely from spring until frost. Autumn sage boasts dozens of small sparkling blooms in magenta, red and coral, or white. It is winter hardy to Zone 8.

A hybrid salvia of debated parentage, Indigo Spires gets rave reviews from gardeners for its rich, royal purple flowers that stand tall above leafy green foliage. Plants grow 3 to 6 feet tall; the flower stalks elongate (about 18 to 20 inches) and deepen in color as autumn approaches. Indigo Spires is winter hardy to Zone 8.

Mealycup sage *(Salvia farinacea)* may be one of the best-known perennial salvias, especially in the lower South. It can survive the winter as far north as Zone 7; give it plenty of time to come back from the root in the spring before declaring it lost. Gardeners who live farther north grow it as an annual, enjoying continuous flowers from May until frost. Victoria is a hardy selection with rich, deep blue flowers. The plants will grow about 18 inches tall and bloom all summer long. The bicolored Strata is an All-America Selections winner. White Bedder adds a cool white to the garden. To keep this salvia from getting leggy, trim blossoms as they fade, cutting back 1 or 2 inches from the tip of the stem. With extra watering, it will continue blooming through fall. This salvia does double duty as a cut flower—fresh or dried.

Pineapple sage *(Salvia elegans)* is appreciated for its lipstick-colored flowers as well as for the fruity fragrance of its leaves and flowers, which can be used fresh or dried in cakes, teas, and herb seasonings. A tender perennial, it grows as an upright shrub 3 to 5 feet tall. Like Mexican bush sage, this salvia waits until early fall for a floral display, but it puts on a grand finale until summer. It should return from its roots in spring in Zone 8 and farther south. You can easily make cuttings and overwinter them indoors for planting outdoors next spring. In the Gulf South, cut plants back to the ground after frost and mulch heavily to protect from winter frost.

Autumn sage has brilliant magenta flowers in the fall.

Harvest, Storage, and Use

Most ornamental salvias are used primarily as landscape plants, for cut flowers, or as sources of nectar for bees, hummingbirds, and butterflies. Pineapple sage is edible; its foliage, which imparts a light pineapple flavor, is popular in fruit salads, on cantaloupe, and in teas, punches, coolers, cakes, and jellies. The leaves also can be dried for future use. Use pineapple sage blossoms in herbal vinegars for a rich red color. Mealycup sage makes an excellent dried flower; the longer you wait to pick this blue-flowered salvia, the sturdier the stems become. Mexican bush sage is an unusually pretty cut flower (hang bouquets upside down in a breezeway to dry them to perfection).

Troubleshooting

Pests and disease problems are minimal, although whiteflies may bother large-flowered types such as anise sage.

Mealycup sage, with both white and deep purple selections, and yellow coreopsis create a colorful combination.

Savory

Summer savory sports small pink blooms in summer. Prune it regularly to prolong its harvest season.

AT A GLANCE

SUMMER SAVORY
Satureja hortensis

Features: delicate herb with narrow, aromatic leaves and small pinkish white flowers

Uses: culinary, landscaping

Type: annual

Height: 1½ feet

Width: 1 foot

Light: full sun to partial shade

Soil: average, well drained, pH 6.8

Water: medium

Range: Zones 4 to 10

Pests: none specific

Remarks: flowers and goes to seed quickly

There are two types of savory. Summer savory is a fast-growing annual that provides a quick, abundant supply of leaves. Winter savory has a stronger flavor, is a perennial evergreen, and can be lightly harvested year-round. Known as the "green bean herb," both types of savory are used to flavor snap beans and navy beans.

In the Landscape

Summer savory (*Satureja hortensis*) grows quickly to reach a height of 18 inches. It has narrow, intensely aromatic leaves on short, branching stems. In summer, small pinkish white flowers appear, attracting bees. Plant summer savory in an herb garden or in a bed with summer annuals, where it will be replaced with a cool-weather annual when it is killed by frost. The herb will also grow in containers.

Winter savory (*Satureja montana*) has shiny, dark green, pointed leaves and a low, sprawling growth habit, reaching 1 foot in height. Dwarf winter savory (*Satureja montana Pygmaea*) grows only 4 inches tall and is good for containers. Winter savory blooms about a month earlier than summer savory; the small lilac or white flowers attract bees. In fall, the herb turns a reddish color. Planted in groups of three to five, winter savory adds color to the landscape in winter; it is also used in edgings, borders, and knot gardens. Winter savory is a perennial and remains evergreen during mild winters in the South. However, in Florida it may die during warm, wet summers.

Planting and Care

Plant summer savory in full sun to partial shade in the spring after threat of frost has passed. It needs well-drained soil with a pH of 6.8; keep the bed moist, as summer savory will die back in dry soil.

Summer savory is easy to grow from seed. Start seeds indoors two to four weeks before the last expected frost, and set the plants out when they are four weeks old. Or sow seeds directly in the garden after frost, sowing only ⅛ inch deep. When seedlings are 2 to 3 inches tall, thin to 10 to 12 inches. To have cuttings for the kitchen all summer, make several successive sowings three weeks apart. To provide support for the weak stems, set forked twigs and small branches next to the plants after thinning.

The easiest way to start winter savory is from transplants set out in spring or fall. Plant them in full sun to partial shade, spacing them 10 to 12 inches apart. Winter savory requires light, well-drained soil with a pH of 6.7 to 7.3; it does best in soil that is slightly poor and dry. If the soil is too rich, plants will be succulent and will not survive the winter; wet soil promotes root rot. Work sand into rich soil and clay to make them lighter and to provide good drainage.

Plants need little care beyond pruning of woody growth in spring to keep plants compact and neat looking. Frequent light harvesting helps maintain a constant supply of tender new growth. Plants will begin to decline after several years, so replace them every two to three years. Winter savory can also be propagated by taking cuttings from side shoots, by dividing clumps in fall or early spring, or by layering. (See page 32 for more about propagation.)

Harvest, Storage, and Use

Summer savory can be harvested when the plant is only 6 inches tall. It grows quickly, so pinch the plant back frequently to encourage it to sprout new leaves and remain bushy. In the Gulf South, summer savory goes to seed rapidly, shortening the harvest period.

Harvest sprigs of winter savory whenever you need them. For major harvests, cut the plant back in mid- to late summer before the plant starts to flower. Do not cut winter savory heavily in late fall.

Both savories have a peppery flavor. Summer savory, the milder of the two, is not available year-round and does not retain its flavor when dried. Winter savory is stronger and more pungent; the soft, new growth has the best flavor. In addition, winter savory retains its flavor well when dried. Both savories can be frozen or stored in vinegar.

Evergreen winter savory is as ornamental as it is flavorful.

GREEN BEANS WITH ONION AND SAVORY

1¼ pounds fresh green beans
2 tablespoons chopped fresh savory
½ cup vertically sliced purple onion

2 teaspoons olive oil
¼ teaspoon salt
Dash freshly ground pepper

Wash green beans; trim ends, and remove strings. Arrange green beans in a steamer basket over boiling water; sprinkle savory over beans. Cover and steam 20 minutes or until crisp-tender. Combine bean mixture, onion, and remaining ingredients in a medium bowl; toss gently. Serve warm. Yield: 5 servings.

AT A GLANCE
❖
WINTER SAVORY
Satureja montana

Features: low-growing shrub useful in borders and knot gardens
Uses: culinary, landscaping
Type: perennial
Height: 1 foot
Width: 6 to 10 inches
Light: full sun to partial shade
Soil: light, dry, well drained, pH 6.7 to 7.3
Water: medium
Range: Zones 6 to 9
Pests: root rot
Remarks: moist or rich soil causes rot

Sorrel

Harvest whole sorrel leaves as you need them. The best flavor comes from young leaves harvested in spring or fall.

An attractive, leafy green plant, sorrel is no longer considered solely a culinary herb. The perennial is also used as an ornamental in herb and salad gardens. Prized by French cooks, sorrel's sour, citruslike flavor is a tangy addition to soups, sauces, and salads. The pretty leaves can enhance fresh herb arrangements.

In the Landscape

The 8-inch-long, lance-shaped leaves of French sorrel grow from the base of the plant and form a rosette that reaches about 2 feet tall. A hardy perennial, sorrel usually dies back in winter and returns in spring. Plant sorrel as a background for flowering herbs or annuals, or use it as an edging herb, keeping it clipped back. In midsummer, small, rust-colored, disk-shaped flowers appear on stalks. These flowers are not showy, and you can cut them as they appear.

Planting and Care

French sorrel will take full sun, but if it is grown in partial shade, the leaves may be more tender. Perennial through Zone 5, the leaves will freeze in winter but will return from the roots after the weather warms. In Zones 7 and south, the leaves are usually evergreen.

You can easily start sorrel from purchased plants or seed sown directly in the garden. Plant in the fall, four weeks before the first frost; or sow seed in spring, several weeks before the last expected frost. Cover seeds with ½ inch of soil. When seedlings are 1 to 2 inches tall, thin to 12 inches. You can also start French sorrel from divisions made in spring or fall. (See page 32 for more about propagation.)

Sorrel likes rich, well-drained, moist soil with a pH of 5.5 to 6.0. Add a slow-release fertilizer to the soil before or during planting. After this, French sorrel will need little care. Hot weather causes it to bloom in spring, so cut back the leaves and flower stalks to the ground and feed with liquid 20-20-20 fertilizer diluted at half the amount recommended in the label directions. The roots will send up tender new leaves.

Harvest outside leaves frequently to promote new growth. Remove flower stalks as they appear so that energy is directed to the production of foliage. If sorrel is allowed to set seed, it will self-sow, and the seedlings can be difficult to eliminate from the garden.

Species and Selections

French sorrel (*Rumex scutatus*) is the preferred selection because its leaves are broader and fleshier and have a finer flavor than other selections.

AT A GLANCE

❖

FRENCH SORREL
Rumex scutatus

Features: attractive, leafy green herb often used in French cooking

Uses: culinary, landscaping

Type: perennial

Height: 2 feet

Width: 1 foot

Light: full sun to partial shade

Soil: rich, moist, well drained, pH 5.5 to 6.0

Water: medium

Range: Zones 5 to 9

Pests: caterpillars, slugs

Remarks: needs little care

Broad-leafed garden sorrel *(Rumex acetosa)* is commonly used in cooking. Although its flavor is not as strong, it is often substituted for French sorrel when that herb is not available. Broad-leafed garden sorrel grows to 3 feet tall with thin, oblong, lancelike leaves. Although almost tasteless in early spring, it becomes more sour and acidic later in the season. It is widely adaptable and will thrive in ordinary or even poor soil, but it requires plenty of moisture. Dig up garden sorrel every three to five years and replant. It requires much the same care as French sorrel and, like French sorrel, can be propagated by seeds and divisions.

Harvest, Storage, and Use

Harvest whole leaves from the rosette as you need them; flavor is best during spring and fall when the weather is cool. Sorrel has a robust spinach-and-lemon flavor. Young leaves in the center of the rosette are less acidic and are best for use in salads and sandwiches. For cooking, cut or pinch off the outer leaves of the plant and leave the young growth in the center. After a summer harvest, cut the plant to the ground to encourage new growth for a fall crop.

Sorrel leaves wilt quickly after harvest, so do not cut leaves until you are ready to use them. Remove the stem and the tough **midrib,** the central leaf vein, before adding the leaves to dishes. Add the leaves at the last minute, and cook them quickly so that their flavor is not lost. Sorrel is very acidic; do not cook the herb in iron pots or it will become discolored. It is best used fresh, but it can also be frozen. Drying does not preserve the flavor well.

Use finely chopped sorrel in soups, salads, creamy sauces, and egg, cheese, and fish dishes, as well as taco and sandwich toppings. Combine it with cooked spinach, or mix it into vegetables or meat pâté. Sorrel can also be used as a salt substitute.

Troubleshooting

Sorrel occasionally attracts caterpillars or slugs that eat holes in the leaves. See pages 124 and 125 for more about these pests.

Sorrel forms a rosette of leaves with a sharp lemon flavor.

SORREL SOUP

3 cups canned ready-to-serve chicken broth
1 cup chopped onion
½ cup long-grain rice, uncooked
2 cloves garlic, minced
3 cups thinly sliced sorrel leaves, loosely packed
¼ teaspoon pepper
1½ cups plain yogurt (at room temperature)
Garnish: chopped fresh parsley

Combine first 4 ingredients in a large saucepan. Bring to a boil; cover, reduce heat, and simmer 12 to 15 minutes or until rice is tender.

Add sorrel and pepper; cook 1 minute or until sorrel wilts.

Gradually add ¾ cup of broth mixture to yogurt, stirring constantly with a wire whisk. Return yogurt mixture to pan. Cook 1 minute or until thoroughly heated. Garnish, if desired. Yield: 5 cups.

Tansy

A cheerful, drought-tolerant perennial, tansy embellishes the herb garden with bright yellow, button-shaped flowers and lush green, fernlike foliage. Native to Europe, tansy was used by the Elizabethans as an insect repellent and an air freshener because of its pungent pine scent. One of the bitter herbs of the Bible, tansy is now considered dangerous to eat and is grown strictly as an ornamental and as a source of cut and dried flowers for herb crafts. Hardy, attractive, and easy to grow, tansy is a good plant for beginning gardeners.

In the Landscape

In a bed or border, pair tansy with silver- and gray-leafed herbs, where its yellow flowers can shine and its fine green foliage takes on a luster. Taller selections grow 3 to 4 feet tall and should be planted at the back of the border. More compact forms make good informal edging plants, with their foliage softening the lines of a walkway. Tansy spreads easily by rhizomes and will naturalize in a wildflower garden. It can also be used as a summer ground cover, especially in a spot of its own where it can spread with abandon. Try a large container on steps near an entryway where visitors can enjoy the spicy aroma of tansy's foliage.

Planting and Care

Plant tansy in full sun to partial shade. Give it a rich, well-drained soil with a pH of 6.0 to 7.0. Add a slow-release fertilizer before or during planting. Tansy prefers slightly dry soil; it can rot in soggy soil.

The easiest way to start tansy is from transplants. Set out transplants in late spring after threat of frost has passed. Or grow your own transplants from seed in spring. Start seed indoors in early spring, and set out the seedlings in late spring after the last frost.

AT A GLANCE
❖
TANSY
Tanacetum vulgare

Features: fernlike ornamental herb with yellow flowers
Uses: crafts, landscaping
Type: perennial
Height: 3 to 4 feet
Width: 2 feet
Light: full sun to partial shade
Soil: rich, well drained, pH 6.0 to 7.0
Water: medium
Range: Zones 4 to 8
Pests: none specific
Remarks: easy to grow, spreads by rhizomes

Another option is to sow seeds directly in the garden in spring or fall. You may also start new tansy plants from divisions from an existing plant. The best time to divide is in the fall. (See page 32 for more about propagation.)

Tansy begins blooming in mid- to late summer. You may need to stake plants after a rainstorm. Or you may consider growing tansy inside a circular plant support such as that used to hold the heavy stems of a peony.

Species and Selections

Fern-leaf tansy *(Tanacetum vulgare var. crispum)* is one of the preferred selections for landscaping because of its neat, dense, rich foliage. How-

ever, it may not bloom as profusely as other tansy selections. Silver Feather *(Tanacetum ptarmiciflorum)* has light gray leaves that appear almost white in the sunlight. It is popular as an accent plant and as an alternative to dusty miller, a common gray-leafed annual. It grows 1 to 2 feet tall and is propagated from seed or cuttings. Silver Feather is winter hardy only in Zone 8 and south but can be grown as an annual farther north.

Harvest, Storage, and Use

Tansy flowers are featured in flower arrangements and wreaths because they hold their form and color well. Pick them when their color is brightest or just before they are fully opened. Remove the leaves and hang bunched flowers upside down to air-dry. (See page 39 for more on drying herbs.)

The deep green foliage of fern-leaf tansy provides a lush backdrop for other plants, such as marigolds and creeping thyme.

Tarragon

French tarragon's leaves have a bittersweet, peppery scent with a hint of anise.

Freshly snipped French tarragon is prized for its rich, cool anise flavor. Try it in a tarragon vinegar for fresh salads or in tarragon butter for basting a roast chicken. A native of Siberia, French tarragon is a hardy perennial. In climates with hot, humid summers, tarragon is a challenge to grow, but it will always thrive in the mild weather of spring and fall, even if it must be replanted as an annual.

In the Landscape

French tarragon has long, thin, dark green leaves and a fine texture. It grows about 2 feet tall with an erect shrubby habit. However, the plant has a tendency to sprawl if left untrimmed. The aromatic leaves grow to 3 inches long; the plant rarely produces a flower.

Planting and Care

French tarragon grows best in Zones 4 through 6, although it may need a protective mulch in winter. In Zone 7 and farther south, tarragon may not do well in the garden because winters are too mild for the plant to go dormant; plants are also bothered by summer heat.

French tarragon prefers full sun but will need partial shade in warmer areas. The herb requires rich, light soil with a pH of 6.0 to 7.3; good drainage is essential because plants are susceptible to root rot in soggy soil. In areas with heavy clay, plant tarragon in a raised bed containing a soil mix of 1 part topsoil, 1 part builder's sand, and 1 part organic matter.

TARRAGON VINEGAR

1 cup chopped fresh tarragon
3¾ cups white wine vinegar or rice vinegar
Fresh tarragon sprigs (optional)

Place chopped tarragon in wide-mouth glass jars. Place vinegar in a medium saucepan; bring to a boil. Pour vinegar over chopped tarragon; cover with metal lids, and screw bands tight. Let stand at room temperature for 2 weeks. Strain vinegar into decorative jars, discarding herb residue; add additional sprigs of fresh tarragon, if desired. Seal jars with a cork or other airtight lid. Yield: 4 cups.

Add a slow-release fertilizer to the soil at planting time and again the following spring.

Start with large transplants or gallon-sized plants, as the larger plants are more successful. True French tarragon is only available as a transplant. To ensure continued vigor in areas where the plant is perennial, divide every third year in early spring by separating the underground runners. Replant the divisions, spacing them 18 inches apart.

Many gardeners, particularly those in Zone 7 and farther south, find that the best way to grow tarragon is in a clay pot or a wire basket lined with sphagnum peat moss. This permits excellent drainage and good air circulation. Plants in containers benefit from afternoon shade during the hottest summer months. During summer, keep soil moist, but you may need to move plants if they are receiving too much water during extended rainy weather.

In winter, move plants to a cold frame or a sunny window. Tarragon needs lots of winter light, but be careful not to overwater the herb during the winter months.

Propagate tarragon by taking cuttings in midsummer. These will root in about two months. Keep them in a greenhouse or cold frame through the first winter. (See page 32 for more about propagation.)

Species and Selections

Russian tarragon (*Artemisia drancunculus Redowskii*) is sometimes offered as a substitute for French tarragon in catalogs but is not recommended for culinary use. Its leaves are slightly aromatic but have no flavor. This tarragon is easy to grow and produces many seeds, unlike French tarragon, which rarely blooms; most tarragon seed sold is Russian tarragon seed.

A native of Mexico and South America, Mexican mint marigold *(Tagetes lucida)* is also called Texas tarragon. Its feathery foliage resembles that of the culinary herb French tarragon. In fact, you can substitute its heat-tolerant, anise-scented leaves for French tarragon in recipes, especially in areas where French tarragon will not grow. Snip fresh sprigs as needed, beginning in spring. Or simply enjoy the color and form of this handsome herb, which bursts into a mass of sunny yellow blooms atop 1- to 2-foot-tall stems in the fall. Although grown as an annual in most of the country, Mexican mint marigold behaves as a half-hardy perennial in Zone 8 and farther south. In south Florida and Texas, it never dies down. In areas with hard winters, grow it as an annual planted in spring.

The yellow flowers of Mexican mint marigold are a showy addition to the fall garden.

AT A GLANCE
❖
MEXICAN MINT MARIGOLD
Tagetes lucida

Features: aromatic foliage and yellow blooms

Uses: landscaping

Type: annual in Zones 4 to 7, perennial in Zones 8 to 10

Height: 2 feet

Width: 1 foot

Light: full sun to partial shade

Soil: loose, well drained, pH 6.0 to 6.8

Water: medium

Range: Zones 4 to 10

Pests: none specific

Remarks: spectacular fall flowering herb

BÉARNAISE SAUCE

¼ cup Tarragon Vinegar (page 116)
¼ cup dry white wine
¼ cup finely chopped shallots
3 egg yolks, lightly beaten
2 tablespoons chopped fresh tarragon
½ cup butter or margarine, cut into thirds

Combine first 3 ingredients in a small saucepan. Bring mixture to a boil over medium heat; reduce heat, and simmer, uncovered, until mixture is reduced to 1 tablespoon (about 10 minutes). Pour mixture through a wire-mesh strainer, reserving liquid and discarding solids. Cool reserved liquid slightly.

Combine reserved liquid, egg yolks, and tarragon in a small saucepan. Add one-third of butter; cook over low heat, stirring constantly with a wire whisk, until butter melts.

Add another third of butter, stirring constantly; as sauce thickens, stir in remaining butter. Cook, stirring constantly, until thickened. Serve immediately. Yield: ¾ cup.

Mexican mint marigold is easy to start from seed or from transplants. It will grow in full sun or partial shade but demands loose, well-drained soil with a pH of 6.0 to 6.8; add a slow-release fertilizer to the soil before or during planting. Once established, it spreads by rhizomes. Propagate new plants to bring indoors for winter by rooting the stems in soil or water. Seedlings may sprout in the garden the following year as the plants reseed.

Harvest, Storage, and Use

Snip fresh sprigs of tarragon as you need them. In spring and again in fall before frost, harvest the entire plant by cutting it to 3 inches above the ground. Lightly harvest again in late spring or early summer to stimulate new growth. Handle leaves carefully, as they bruise. French tarragon can be dried but does not always hold its flavor well; it is best preserved in vinegar or butter, or frozen. French tarragon loses its flavor and becomes bitter when heated, so add it in the last 10 to 15 minutes of the cooking process.

Use Mexican mint marigold as you would tarragon. Flowers are edible; use these or a light sprinkling of petals as a garnish. The blooms also make striking cut flowers.

Finely chopped French tarragon or Mexican mint marigold adds a distinctive mild flavor to soups, sauces, marinades, green salads, fruit, poultry, seafood, vegetables, and egg dishes. Mix the herb with cream or cottage cheese, sour cream, yogurt or mayonnaise (for chicken salad), or béarnaise sauce. Tarragon butter is simple to make and can be stored in the freezer. For each 2 teaspoons of softened butter, add 1 teaspoon finely chopped tarragon. Add fresh lemon juice and salt to taste.

Troubleshooting

Tarragon is susceptible to root rot and powdery mildew, especially if the soil is wet or too acidic. Tarragon can also attract mealybugs and whiteflies. See pages 124-125 for more about these pests.

Thyme

Upright types of thyme, such as this English thyme, grow into small, finely textured shrubs. Clip them regularly to keep the plants vigorous.

Walk across a carpet of thyme, and you will understand why European settlers brought it to the United States and why it continues to be one of the most beloved herbs in the garden. The aroma is warm and exotic; the foliage is finely textured. While some selections of thyme are essential in the kitchen, others are among the most appealing herbs for landscaping. The upright types grow into small shrubs, while the creeping ones contain a variety of flower and foliage colors. Thyme is evergreen throughout much of the South—you can harvest culinary types for soups, stews, stocks, bouquets garnis, vegetables, and meat dishes all winter long.

In the Landscape

No matter what the season, thyme puts on a show. Its evergreen foliage provides anchor in an herb garden in winter and varies in color from dark green to silver and gold to variegated. In early spring, the flowers open, sprinkling the plant with spots of white, pink, lavender, or rose.

Use shrublike upright selections in borders or as small hedges. Plant creeping selections as edgings or ground covers, between paving stones, or along rock walls. No other herb serves to soften hard lines or angles as well as thyme does. Thyme also makes an ideal container plant. It is drought tolerant and thrives in the superior soil and good drainage provided in a container.

Planting and Care

Thyme does best in full sun to partial shade, but not in deep shade. It is easiest to start from transplants set out in the fall or in spring as soon as the soil warms. Seeds of most selections do not germinate easily and are difficult to handle because of their small size.

Plant thyme in light, well-drained soil with a pH of 6.0 to 6.7. Add a slow-release fertilizer to the soil before or during planting and again each spring. Thyme must have excellent drainage to succeed in the South. Mulch to conserve moisture, but add a ring of builder's

---

AT A GLANCE

❖

THYME
Thymus species

Features: evergreen, upright or creeping herb with flavorful foliage

Uses: crafts, culinary, landscaping

Type: perennial

Height: 3 to 12 inches

Width: 4 to 12 inches

Light: full sun to partial shade

Soil: average, light, well drained, pH 6.0 to 6.7

Water: medium

Range: Zones 5 to 9

Pests: fungus, root rot, spider mites

Remarks: wide range of landscape and culinary uses

Bring color to your patio with a collection of different thymes, flowering dianthus, and other low-growing herbs.

sand around the crown to prevent root rot. With a layer of protective mulch, most selections of upright thyme are cold hardy through Zone 5. However, do not mulch mat-forming types or they will rot.

Propagate thyme by stem cuttings or by divisions in fall or early spring. Creeping selections can also be propagated by layering. (See page 32 for more about propagation.)

Given proper growing conditions, thyme will need little care besides a regular light pruning, starting in the spring, to prevent it from becoming woody and brittle. Prune upright selections by one-third in spring to keep them shapely. Creeping types often become ragged in winter; if this happens, cut them back to the ground in late winter before spring growth begins.

Species and Selections

There are dozens of selections of thyme. The basic difference between them is that some are grown for culinary use and others are used primarily in landscaping. Both types are edible, but creeping thymes are usually small and tedious to harvest and are therefore more valuable as ground covers.

Garden thyme *(Thymus vulgaris),* also known as common, English, or French thyme, is most often used as a seasoning. The flavor of this hardy perennial is pungent and strong. Plants grow upright and range in height from 8 to 12 inches depending on the selection. Trim plants to keep them neat and to prevent them from getting too woody. English thyme has dark green, oval leaves, and French thyme has narrow gray leaves.

One of the most popular culinary thymes, lemon thyme *(Thymus serpyllum)* is known for its enticing lemon scent and taste. Sometimes listed in catalogs as *Thymus* x *citriodorus,* it is a hardy perennial that grows 4 to 12 inches tall. Leaves may be green or edged in yellow, depending on the selection. Lemon thyme spreads rapidly and bears pinkish flowers in summer. The green form is the best for culinary use.

Known for its beautiful rose-purple flowers that bloom in early summer, caraway thyme *(Thymus herba-barona)* has a mild caraway flavor. It is a hardy perennial that grows 2 to 5 inches tall, with narrow green leaves.

Golden thyme is a popular creeping ornamental.

Caraway has a neat growth habit that requires minimal pruning; however, the plant spreads rapidly.

Mother-of-thyme *(Thymus praecox Arcticus)*, also called creeping thyme, grows 3 to 5 inches tall and is used primarily as an ornamental. It has tiny oval leaves and bears purple flowers in early summer. Plants spread by rhizomes. Cut this selection to the ground in spring to get rid of the ragged growth left from winter. Mother-of-thyme is not reliably hardy north of Zone 7. There are a number of selections with different flower and leaf colors.

Harvest, Storage, and Use

Harvest thyme leaves as you need them. The flavor is most concentrated just before plants bloom. Strip leaves from woody stems before using. Keep the stems on coals when grilling to add flavor to foods.

Because thyme usually stays green through the winter, it does not need to be preserved. But for convenience, thyme can be easily dried, stored in oil, stored in vinegar, refrigerated, or frozen. Let the foliage air-dry. Store in an airtight container.

Make thyme butter for basting seafood, chicken, or pork. (See page 36 for information on making herb butters.) Add thyme to mayonnaise (2 tablespoons fresh chopped thyme to 1 cup mayonnaise) for sandwiches or to dried beans, meat stews, or vegetables, such as cabbage. Use it to flavor rice or new potatoes (along with garlic, butter, and Parmesan cheese). Add thyme to any slow-cooked dish (especially soups and stews) and to sautéed vegetables, broiled or roasted meat or poultry, breads, and sauces.

Thyme is also one of the best herbs to use for wreaths and other crafts.

Troubleshooting

Thyme can suffer from root rot and fungal diseases if not given proper drainage. The herb also attracts spider mites. See pages 124-125 for more about these diseases and pests.

THYME RICE

2 cups water
1 cup long-grain rice, uncooked
2 teaspoons butter or margarine
1½ teaspoons beef-flavored bouillon granules
1 teaspoon Worcestershire sauce
1 teaspoon chopped fresh chives
1 to 1½ teaspoons chopped fresh thyme
½ teaspoon minced garlic

Combine all ingredients in a heavy saucepan. Bring to a boil; stir well. Reduce heat, cover, and simmer for 20 minutes or until rice is done. Yield: 4 servings.

Yarrow

Common yarrow brings deep pink to the color palette of the herb garden.

Once popular for home remedies, yarrow remains a stellar member of the herb garden because of its brightly colored flowers. Yarrow not only blooms a long time, but it also makes an excellent cut flower. In addition, it dries well to become a charming everlasting herb for wreaths, arrangements, and other herbal crafts. Depending on the type, yarrow may bear yellow, pink, white, or maroon flowers.

In the Landscape

Tough and easy to grow, yarrow is a fine ornamental for the herb garden, with gray or green fernlike foliage that is attractive even when the plants are not in bloom. Plants range from 2 to 5 feet tall, depending on the selection. Use them at the back of flower or herb borders, in a meadow, or as mass plantings in full sun. Common yarrow is native to Europe but has naturalized in the United States and may be seen growing in sunny areas along roadsides. It is an excellent plant for areas with poor soil. For a mix of color and texture, try combining yellow selections with purple basil or blue or purple salvia. Yarrow's blooms of red or pink complement gray-leafed herbs, such as lavender or sage.

Planting and Care

Yarrow withstands heat and drought but cannot tolerate hot, humid weather. It needs bright sunshine, excellent drainage, and good air circulation to help protect its foliage from humid weather.

Start yarrow from transplants set out in spring or fall. Plant in an area with light, well-drained soil that has a pH of 6.0 to 6.7. Good drainage is especially important in winter, when yarrow is most susceptible to root rot. Add builder's sand and organic matter to the soil, and consider planting yarrow in a raised bed. To help young plants get started in poor soil, feed them with a slow-release fertilizer. However, do not overfertilize, as yarrow does better in soil that is not too rich. Fern-leaf yarrow may require staking if planted in rich soil or overfertilized, while common yarrow will spread beyond control.

Divide yarrow every two to three years in spring or fall to rejuvenate the plant and prevent crowding. *Deadheading*, or removing spent blossoms, will help keep the plant blooming all summer. Yarrow attracts beneficial insects, such as butterflies and ladybugs, so leave a few blooms for them to eat.

AT A GLANCE

❖

YARROW
Achillea species

Features: fernlike herb with bright flower clusters

Uses: crafts, landscaping

Type: perennial

Height: 2 to 5 feet

Width: 1 foot

Light: full sun

Soil: average, light, well drained, pH 6.0 to 6.7

Water: medium

Range: Zones 3 to 8

Pests: root rot and stem rot

Remarks: multiplies easily, needs excellent drainage

Species and Selections

Fern-leaf yarrow *(Achillea filipendulina)* grows 3 to 5 feet tall; its fernlike, handsome foliage ranges from gray-green to silver, depending on the selection. The main flush of yellow blooms appears in late May or early June and lasts about a month. Sporadic blooms appear throughout the summer if the old flowers are kept cut. Hardy from Zone 3 to 7, recommended hybrid selections include Coronation Gold (about 3 feet tall) and Moonshine (about 1½ to 2 feet tall). Propagate by division in fall or spring. Coronation Gold is preferred for drying and using in crafts. The only drawback to fern-leaf yarrow and some of its hybrids is that they have problems with rot and leaf diseases in the hot, humid coastal South.

Common yarrow *(Achillea millefolium)* has fresh fernlike green foliage that often remains through winter in the lower South. Ranging from 1 to 2 feet tall, common yarrow blooms from late spring to summer and occasionally again in the fall. Some consider common yarrow a weed, as it has naturalized in the wild and will spread in the garden via runners and seedlings. However, if divided regularly in the fall and not overfertilized, common yarrow will remain compact. It is the best yarrow for the lower and coastal South, as it tolerates heat and drought. It is also more tolerant of humid weather than fern-leaf yarrow. Recommended selections include Cerise Queen, Fire King, and Lavender Lady. Plants in the Galaxy series do not spread as readily; flowers are white, salmon, rosy pink, or deep red.

Harvest, Storage, and Use

Yarrow is a choice cut flower to use fresh or dried. For drying and preserving, cut the flowers when they are completely open. Use a rubber band to bind the ends of the stems together, and hang the bunch upside down in a dry, dark place. Or hang stems singly for better flower shape. The flowers will be ready for arranging in three to four weeks. The foliage of yarrow is aromatic and can be dried and used in potpourris and moth repellents.

Troubleshooting

Fern-leaf yarrow is susceptible to root rot and stem rot. Provide excellent drainage. In the summer, water yarrow early in the morning to help prevent disease.

Fern-leaf yarrow likes full sun and good drainage. Its flowers are excellent for drying.

White-flowering selections of common yarrow combine with yellow fern-leaf yarrow for a crisp, cool look.

Pests and Diseases

Although most herbs are not troubled by insects and diseases, a few are bothered by those named here. One way to prevent or reduce these problems is to manage your garden in a way that discourages them. Always look for disease-resistant selections that are adapted to your soil and climate. Plant herbs in an open, sunny location where there is good drainage and air circulation to minimize the spread of fungus diseases. And if pests appear, spray with a recommended pesticide at the first sign of infestation.

Aphids

Japanese Beetle

Aphids

Aphids are tiny, pear-shaped insects about ⅛ to ¼ inch long; they are frequently green or black but may also be yellow or pink. They suck sap from the tender young stems and flower buds, causing curled leaves, misshapen growth, and unopened buds. Aphids are usually worst in the spring and fall. They will produce hundreds of offspring in a few weeks, so it is crucial to control them as soon as they appear.

Japanese Beetles

These ½-inch metallic green and copper beetles often fly into your yard from elsewhere and are difficult to control. Japanese beetles like to chew a bit and fly to another plant, making it hard to control them. They usually feed in hordes with hundreds present at one time. Dusting foliage with a recommended pesticide helps, but you must keep the dust on new growth as it unfurls. The best way to control Japanese beetles is to kill the grubs, or larvae, which feed in lawns.

Mealybugs

Mealybugs are soft-bodied insects that are about ¼ inch long and are covered with a white, cottony looking wax. Some species have three tail-like projections. They suck sap from tender young leaves and stems, causing deformed foliage.

Powdery Mildew

Powdery mildew is a disease that looks like white to gray dust growing on the surface of the leaves. It will cause the leaves to dry and wither thus weakening the plant. To prevent powdery mildew, give plants good air circulation to keep the foliage dry so that the mildew cannot develop. The best way to control the disease is to spray both sides of the leaves with an approved fungicide before it appears; this will be difficult unless you have seen it in your garden before and can predict its occurrence, usually in spring and fall. Once the mildew appears, it is harder to control.

Root Rot and Stem Rot

Rots associated with poor drainage and humidity are the most frequent problem with herbs. Affected plants decline as their roots begin to rot or as their stems rot and die back. As a preventive measure, plant herbs in well-drained soil and provide good air circulation.

Slugs

Slugs are like snails without shells. They chew holes in the leaves and flowers of young plants. Slugs feed at night, so it will be difficult to see them during the day. One sure sign of slugs is a shiny slime trail on the leaves in your garden. You can control slugs with bait, but read the warning label carefully, as most are poisonous to pets.

Southern Blight

Silver-leafed herbs, such as artemisia, lavender, and sage, are susceptible to a soil-borne fungus known as Southern Blight. Infected leaves turn black and drop from the plant; infected stems die back. As a preventive measure, sprinkle a half-inch layer of builder's sand around the plants so that the surface around them dries more quickly.

Spider Mites

Spider mites are tiny, spiderlike insects that collect on the underside of leaves and on flower buds, sucking sap from the plants. They are worst during dry weather in spring and fall. You may not see mites until their feeding begins to make the topside of the leaves look faded and mottled. If you turn a leaf over, you can see clusters of pinpoint-sized spider mites and perhaps a delicate webbing. To control spider mites, spray the underside of the leaves.

Whiteflies

These white, mothlike insects are only ⅛ inch long, and you can usually see them on the underside of young leaves. If you shake the plant, they will fly out, and then light again. They suck sap from the leaves, leaving foliage yellowed and spotted. To control whiteflies, spray the underside of the leaves.

Powdery Mildew

Slug

Spider mite damage

Index

Index

Special Thanks

Ralph Anderson
Birmingham Botanical Gardens
Nona Hurst
Juanita Martinez
John O'Hagan
Marvin Perry
Howard L. Puckett
Cathy Ritter
Barbara Sanders
Winyss Shepherd
Southern Progress Corporation
  Library Staff